The Rural Route 2 Cookbook

ISBN 978-1-60145-592-5

Published by LeAnn R. Ralph, Colfax, Wisconsin, USA.

Printed in the United States of America.

Booklocker.com, Inc.
2008

The Rural Route 2 Cookbook

Tried and True Recipes from Wisconsin Farm Country

LeAnn R. Ralph

Dedication

For all of those who grew up on farms or who visited aunts and uncles,
grandmas and grandpas or cousins who lived down on the farm.

And in memory of my mother and father, who were farmers all their lives.
Dad worked hard every single day on our small family dairy farm in west central Wisconsin.
He didn't need "fancy food." He wanted good food. And lots of it.
Like Dad used to say, "If you don't eat, you can't work."
Of course, he also used to say, "If you don't work, you can't eat."

****

Foreword

The recipes in this book use ingredients that you probably already have in your cupboard or ingredients that you can find easily at any grocery store.

Most of the recipes are fairly easy, too.
Like I always say, "If it's not easy—I don't do it!"

LeAnn R. Ralph
Colfax, Wisconsin

Table of Contents

Beverages

Frosty Cranberry Pineapple Punch

This recipe makes between 5 and 6 quarts of punch. A delicious way to cool off on a hot summer afternoon—plus, it makes enough to serve at your Fourth of July party or other summer parties. Also, cranberries contain antioxidants. This punch is not only good—it's good for you!

64-ounce bottle of cranberry juice (100 percent juice)
46-ounce (or thereabouts) can of 100 percent pineapple juice drink
2-liter bottle of 7-UP (diet or regular), or Sprite or ginger ale
1 pint of orange or raspberry sherbet

Put the juice and soda pop into the refrigerator for a few hours to chill thoroughly. Then pour the cranberry juice, pineapple juice and soda pop or ginger ale into a very large mixing bowl, a punch bowl or another container (Dutch oven or a large soup kettle) large enough to hold all of the ingredients. Stir thoroughly. Drop the sherbet by spoonfuls into the punch. Enjoy!

****

Fruit Smoothie

This recipe is a great way to cool off on a hot summer day and is quite tasty when you don't feel like eating much. It's good, too, when you've got a cold or the flu because it's easy to swallow and soothes a sore throat.

1/2 cup dry milk
1 cup ice cubes or crushed ice
1 cup water
1 to 2 cups of your favorite fruit (strawberries, raspberries, blueberries, bananas, kiwi, peaches…)
several tablespoons of sugar (if desired)

Pour the ice and water into a blender. Process for a few seconds to crush up the ice. Add the dry milk, fruit and sugar (if desired). Process in the blender until the mixture is smooth.

Note: If you want your smoothie to have a more creamy texture, add additional dry milk by the tablespoon and process. If you want the smoothie to be sweeter, add a little more sugar. Add 1 cup of fruit if you want it less fruity, or add more fruit if you want more fruit taste. If the mixture is too thick, add a little more water—or try some 7-Up or gingerale.

****

Hot Apple Cider

Flavored with cinnamon, all-spice and orange, this recipe is sure to please young and old alike. I make this for Christmas when my family is here, and there is usually not much left by the end of the afternoon.

2 bottles of apple juice (46 ounce bottles or thereabouts)
3 cinnamon sticks
8 dried all-spice berries
1 whole orange

Note: Ever since a few people became sick a few years ago from E.coli bacteria in cold-pressed apple cider (from the deer leaving droppings in the orchards), I have used apple juice instead.

Half an hour before your guests will arrive (or a half hour before you want hot apple cider to drink), pour the bottles of apple juice into a large kettle. Add the cinnamon sticks and all-spice berries. Slice up the orange, peeling and all, and put into the kettle with the other ingredients. Heat on a medium setting until the mixture is just starting to simmer and then turn down on low and leave the burner on low to keep the cider hot. After the cider is hot, you can also pour it into a crockpot to keep it hot. Makes approximately 12 servings.

****

Old- Fashioned Hot Cocoa

When I was a kid growing up on our farm, before there were such things as hot cocoa mixes, this is how my mother and my big sister made hot chocolate.

   1/2 cup sugar
   1/3 cup cocoa
   dash of salt
   1 1/2 cups water
   4 cups milk
   1/4 to 1/2 teaspoon vanilla

Mix sugar, cocoa and salt in a saucepan. Gradually stir in water. Heat to boiling, stirring constantly, and boil for a minute or two. Gradually stir in the milk. Heat to almost boiling but do not boil. (If you let the milk boil, you will get a "skin" on top of your cocoa when it begins to cool off.) Stir in the vanilla. Beat with a hand beater or a wire whisk for a minute or so before serving.

If a sweeter drink is desired, stir in another teaspoon or two of sugar after it has been poured into a cup. Add marshmallows if desired.

****

Instant Cocoa Mix

Christmas gift (or birthday gift) idea: Put the cocoa mix into pint jars or half-pint jars. Set the lids on the jars. Place a square of fabric with a holiday pattern (or another pattern) on it over the lid. Screw on the ring. Tie a ribbon around the top of the jar. One recipe makes about four pints.

   6 cups of nonfat dry milk
   1 cup of cocoa powder
   2 cups sugar

Measure all ingredients into a mixing bowl. Stir until thoroughly combined. Store in a covered container.

Use 2 to 4 tablespoons of the mix (to taste) to a cup or a mug of very hot water.

****

Russian Refresher

This is a "lighter" version of Russian Tea because it does not contain instant tea. My mother liked both Russian Refresher and Russian Tea, although she preferred Russian Tea because she liked tea. When she was a girl, her Norwegian mother enjoyed drinking tea.

1/2 teaspoon ground cloves
1 teaspoon ground cinnamon
2 cups powdered orange drink
1/2 cup dry sweetened lemonade mix
1 1/3 cup white sugar

Measure all ingredients into a bowl and mix well. Store in a covered container. Use 1 to 2 teaspoons of the mixture per cup of hot water (or to taste).

****

Russian Tea

1 cup of powdered orange drink
1 cup of sugar
1 teaspoon ground cinnamon
1/2 teaspoon ground cloves
1/2 cup instant tea

Mix the dry ingredients. Store in a jar or another covered container. Use 2 teaspoons of the mix per cup of hot water (or to taste).

****

Gift idea: You can also put the Russian Refresher or Russian Tea into quart, pint or half-pint jars and give as gifts. Decorate the jars as described for the hot cocoa mix.

Lemonade Punch

We make this for our church dinners, and it is very popular with our guests. My big sister used to make a similar drink during the summer as a treat when we needed a break from baling hay.

Lemonade drink mix
7-Up, Sprite or ginger ale
Fruit juice (I like to use 100 percent juice, since we now know that high fructose corn syrup can contribute to problems with diabetes and obesity)

Each gallon of punch serves 16 to 20 people (fewer people if it's a hot summer day).

To make about a gallon of punch:

Mix up 1 quart of lemonade according to the package directions. Add 1 2-liter bottle of 7-Up, Sprite or ginger ale. Stir in 1 bottle (46 ounces or thereabouts) of 100 percent fruit juice. I have used cranberry, apple, pineapple and apricot juice.

To make a lighter version, use sugar free lemonade drink mix and diet 7-Up, Sprite or ginger ale.

****

Breads, Muffins
and
Cinnamon Rolls

Apple Bread

This is my favorite recipe for apple bread. It works well with fresh apples or with frozen apples.

2 cups sugar
1 cup canola oil
4 eggs
2 teaspoons vanilla
1/4 cup sour milk (add 1 teaspoon of vinegar or lemon juice to fresh milk)
1 teaspoon soda
4 cups flour
1 teaspoon salt
1/2 teaspoon cinnamon
4 cups chopped apples
1 cup chopped walnuts (optional)

Measure all ingredients into a mixing bowl and stir until thoroughly combined. Divide the batter between 2 greased loaf pans. For smaller loaves, divide the batter between three or four loaf pans. Bake for 1 hour at 350 degrees Fahrenheit or until the loaves feel set when tapped. At times I have had to bake the loaves for 10 or 15 minutes more. If you are making smaller loaves, you might have to bake the loaves for a shorter period of time (maybe 45 or 50 minutes).

Allow to cool before removing from the pans.

Note: Batter will be stiff.

****

Old-Fashioned Baking Powder Biscuits

I have noticed over the years that there are two philosophies for Strawberry Shortcake. There are the people who make Strawberry Shortcake with biscuits. And then there are those who make it with angel food cake or plain white or yellow cake. My mother belonged to the biscuit philosophy. She also made baking powdered biscuits when she ran out of bread and needed a quick bread to serve with a meal.

My mom and dad both considered baking powder biscuits spread with butter and drizzled with pancake syrup or dark corn syrup to be an extra-special treat.

3 cups flour
1/2 cup shortening
3 teaspoons baking powder
1/2 teaspoon salt
2 teaspoons sugar
1 cup milk

Measure the flour, shortening baking powder, sugar and salt into a mixing bowl. Cut the shortening into the flour with a fork until it resembles coarse meal. Gradually stir in the milk to form the dough. If the dough seems too dry, add milk by tablespoons. If the dough seems too soft, add flour by the quarter cup.

Knead the dough on a floured surface for a minute or so. Then roll out to a half-inch thick and make biscuits with a biscuit cutter or donut cutter or round cookie cutter.

Bake on an ungreased cookie sheet at 350 degrees Fahrenheit for 20 or 25 minutes or until golden brown.

Makes about 12 to 18 biscuits, depending on the size of the cutter you use.

Strawberry Shortcake

4 cups of fresh strawberries (or thawed frozen strawberries)
1 cup of sugar (or to taste)

Crush the strawberries. Stir in the sugar until dissolved. Serve over baking powder biscuits and topped with whipped cream. Yum!

* * * * * * * * * * * * * * * * * * * *

Bread Pudding

When I was a kid, my mother made bread pudding with homemade bread that was a couple of days old. When she was ready to bake another batch of bread, if there was some left from the previous batch, then she would make bread pudding. At other times, the barn kitties would get to eat the leftover bread with fresh, warm milk poured over it at milking time—a kitty cat version of bread pudding, I suppose. If family members turn up their noses at the idea of Bread Pudding, tell them it's French Toast Casserole.

6 cups of bread chunks
4 eggs
1/2 cup brown sugar
1/4 cup white sugar
1 teaspoon vanilla
1/4 teaspoon salt
1/2 teaspoon cinnamon
2 cups milk
1/2 cup to 1 cup raisins (optional)

Grease a 3-quart casserole dish. Tear the bread into chunks and put into the casserole dish. (If you are adding raisins, alternate layers of raisins between the bread.) Put the eggs into a mixing bowl and beat for a minute or so with a fork. Add the brown sugar, white sugar, vanilla, salt and cinnamon. Beat with the fork for several minutes until sugar is beaten into the eggs. Add the milk. Stir thoroughly. Pour over the bread in the casserole dish.

Bake at 350 degrees Fahrenheit for 60 to 70 minutes, or until a knife inserted in the center of the pudding comes out clean. Serve either warm or cold. Good with cream, whipped cream or ice cream! Also good with applesauce, strawberries or blueberries.

****

Casserole Bread
(Easy Bread Recipe!)

This bread recipe — a batter bread that is very easy —is baked in a two-quart casserole.

1 cup warm water
1 package of dry yeast (or 2 teaspoons of bulk yeast)
2/3 cup Canola oil
1 teaspoon of salt
2 eggs
3 cups of flour (to make whole wheat Casserole Bread, use 1 cup of whole wheat flour and 2 cups of white flour)

Dissolve the yeast in the warm water. Add the canola oil, salt, eggs and 1 cup of flour. Use an electric mixer or a whisk to beat until smooth. Add remaining flour. Stir until thoroughly mixed in. Let batter rise in a warm place (with the bowl covered) for 30 minutes.

Stir down dough. Spread in a greased two-quart casserole dish. Cover the dish. Let the dough rise in a warm place for another 30 minutes. Remove the cover.

Bake at 350 degrees Fahrenheit for 40 minutes or until golden brown.

Immediately remove the bread from the casserole. Brush with shortening to keep the crust soft. Cut into slices when the bread is cool.

****

Cinnamon Raisin Bread

My mother loved cinnamon raisin bread. This bread makes great toast for breakfast or is good for snacks. When I make Cinnamon Raisin Bread for coffee after church on Sunday morning, not much comes back home with me!

(This recipe makes 2 large loaves or can be used to make 3 or 4 smaller loaves.)

2 packages of dry yeast (or 4 teaspoons bulk yeast)
3 1/2 cups warm water
2 eggs
1/2 cup sugar
1/2 cup cooking oil (I like to use Canola oil)
1 teaspoon salt
2 cups of raisins
2 teaspoons cinnamon
9 to 10 cups of flour

Dissolve yeast in the warm water. Add eggs, sugar, cooking oil, salt, cinnamon and 3 or 4 cups of flour. Beat until smooth with a whisk or an electric mixer. Add the raisins. Add the remaining flour (enough to make a stiff dough). Knead for 5 or 10 minutes. Place dough in a large, greased bowl, cover, and let rise in a warm place for 45 minutes.

Knead dough for another couple of minutes. Divide in half. Shape each half into a loaf. Grease two loaf pans. Put the dough into the pans. Let rise in a warm place for another 45 minutes.

Bake at 350 degrees Fahrenheit for 35 to 40 minutes or until the loaves are golden brown and sound hollow when tapped.

Remove from oven. Brush with shortening while still hot to keep the crust soft. Allow to cool for 10 minutes and remove from pans. Allow to cool completely before cutting.

****

Cinnamon Roll Muffins

If you love cinnamon rolls but do not have the time or the inclination to make traditional cinnamon rolls with dough that has to rise twice before the cinnamon rolls are baked, try this easy variation for muffins. This was one of Mom's favorite recipes—especially when I made them!

1 cup milk with 1 tablespoon of lemon juice or vinegar added to it
1/2 cup brown sugar
1 teaspoon baking soda
1/2 teaspoon salt
1/2 teaspoon vanilla
1 egg
3 to 3 1/2 cups flour
soft butter
sugar
cinnamon

Pour milk into a measuring cup and add the lemon juice or vinegar. Measure the brown sugar, baking soda, salt, vanilla and egg into a mixing bowl. Add the milk. Add the flour. Stir until thoroughly combined.

Turn the dough out onto a lightly floured surface and knead for a minute or so. Roll the dough into a 12-inch by 24-inch rectangle. Spread with butter. Sprinkle with sugar and cinnamon. Roll the dough into a log beginning at the wide side. Stretch the log slightly. Cut into two-inch pieces and put the pieces into greased muffin tins or muffin tins lined with cupcake papers. (I like to use the cupcake papers because the papers make cleaning the muffin tin that much easier!)

Bake at 375 degrees Fahrenheit for 20 minutes or until golden brown.

Allow the muffins to cool for 5 minutes and then remove them from the muffin tins.

This recipe makes 1 dozen cinnamon roll muffins.

****

Homemade Cinnamon Rolls
(in 2 hours or less!)

If I've heard it once, I've heard it a dozen times: "Make homemade cinnamon rolls? From scratch? Are you crazy? That takes all day!" I have several recipes for homemade cinnamon rolls that do, indeed, take at least all afternoon — scald the milk and let it cool to room temperature (30 minutes); mix the dough and let it raise for an hour (1.5 hours); punch down the dough and let it raise for another hour (1 hour); shape into cinnamon rolls and let raise for another hour (1.5 hours); and then, finally, bake the cinnamon rolls (30 minutes) — for a grand total of 5 hours from start to finish. But it doesn't have to be that way. You really can make homemade cinnamon rolls from scratch in two hours or less. This recipe is one of the most popular ways that people find my website on the Internet (www.ruralroute2.com).

2 cups of warm water
1/2 cup sugar
4 teaspoons dry yeast (or two packages of dry yeast)
2 eggs
1 teaspoon salt
1/3 cup Canola oil (you can use any kind of cooking oil, or shortening if you prefer)
6 to 7 cups of flour

Dissolve the yeast in the warm water. Add the sugar and salt. Mix. Add the cooking oil (or shortening), 2 eggs, 2 cups of flour and beat until smooth. Stir in 3 more cups of flour. Begin kneading the dough, adding the final cup of flour. If the dough seems too sticky, knead in more flour, a quarter to a half cup at a time. Let the dough rest for 20 minutes. (I leave it sitting on the counter and use the time to wash up the bowl and other utensils and to clean off the counter top.)

Roll the dough into a rectangle that's 24 to 30 inches long by about 16 inches wide. Spread with soft butter and sprinkle with cinnamon and sugar (about 1/2 cup sugar and 1 teaspoon of cinnamon). Starting at the wide end, roll into a log. Cut the cinnamon rolls into equal sized slices (approximately one inch wide each or slightly more) and place into two greased 9x13 pans. Put in a warm place to rise for 45 minutes.

Bake at 350 degrees Fahrenheit for 25 minutes (or until the cinnamon rolls are golden brown). Allow to cool for 5 minutes and then turn out of the pans.

This recipes makes two dozen cinnamon rolls. If you want REALLY BIG cinnamon rolls, cut into 12 equal pieces 2 inches wide. Total amount of time needed from start to finish (including time to bake) is about 2 hours.

****

English Muffin Bread
(Easy Batter Bread Recipe)

With this recipe for batter bread, you can have fresh bread to serve in about an hour and a half. It goes well with soup or stew and makes great toast! It also makes good toasted garlic bread to serve with spaghetti. I usually make this recipe without the cornmeal because the cornmeal is so messy when I dump the bread out of the pans. The bread rises while it is baking, but then before it is finished baking, the top falls, so don't be surprised that there's a dip in the middle of the loaves

5 cups of flour
2 packages of dry yeast (or 4 teaspoons bulk yeast)
1 tablespoon sugar
1 teaspoon salt
1/4 teaspoon baking soda
2 cups warm milk
1/2 cup warm water
cornmeal (if desired)

Measure 2 cups of flour, the yeast, sugar, salt and baking powder into a large bowl and stir to combine the dry ingredients. Add the warm milk and water and, with an electric mixer, blend on low speed for a minute, scraping the bowl constantly. Beat on high speed for 3 minutes.

Stir in the remaining flour. If you have dough hooks for your mixer, you might want to use them. If you don't have dough hooks, you might want to consider stirring in the flour by hand because the dough becomes quite stiff.

Grease 2 loaf pans. If you're going to use the cornmeal, sprinkle the greased pans with cornmeal. If you're not going to use the cornmeal, just grease the pans. Divide the batter between the two pans. If you're using the cornmeal, sprinkle cornmeal on top of the dough.

Let rise in a warm place for 45 minutes.

Bake at 375 degrees Fahrenheit for 35 minutes until golden brown. Remove from the pans immediately.

****

Homemade Breadsticks

This recipe for breadsticks is very easy. You can sprinkle them with garlic and serve with spaghetti, or I have also sprinkled them with cinnamon and sugar and made them for breakfast. My husband loves these breadsticks served with spaghetti.

2 to 3 cups flour
1 tablespoon sugar
1 teaspoon baking powder
1/2 teaspoon salt
1 cup milk

Measure all ingredients into a medium mixing bowl and stir until thoroughly combined. If the dough seems too soft, add flour by the 1/4 cup until it reaches a consistency you can roll out.

Roll into a rectangle approximately 10 inches by 10 inches. Cut into sticks (4 inches by 1 inch). Pour enough canola and/or olive oil into a 9x13 pan to cover the bottom (about 1/4 to 1/2 cup; use a pastry brush to spread it around).

Put the breadsticks in the pan. Turn over to coat both sides with oil. Sprinkle with garlic powder (if desired) (or with cinnamon and sugar if you are making them for breakfast). Bake at 400 degrees Fahrenheit for 20 to 25 minutes until golden brown. Makes about 2 dozen breadsticks.

****

Hot Cross Buns

When I was a kid, my mother talked about eating hot cross buns at Easter when she was a child that her mother used to make.

2 packages dry yeast (or 4 teaspoons bulk yeast)
2 cups warm water
1 cup mashed potatoes
1/2 cup sugar
1/2 cup shortening
1 teaspoon salt
2 eggs
1 teaspoon cinnamon
1 cup raisins
5 to 6 cups flour

Dissolve the yeast in warm water. Add the potatoes, sugar, shortening, salt, eggs, cinnamon, raisins and 2 cups of flour. Beat until smooth. Stir in remaining flour. Knead for about 5 minutes. (The dough will be sticky and soft.) Place in a warm place to rise for 1 hour.

Punch down dough. Shape the dough into 24 equal pieces. Place on a greased baking sheet. Let rise for 45 minutes. (My mother said that after the buns are shaped you should cut a cross in the top with a scissors; I've always found that when the buns are finished rising, you can't really see the cross. The buns just end up with four "points" on the top. But you can try it if you want.)

Bake at 350 degrees Fahrenheit for 25 to 30 minutes or until golden brown. When the buns are completely cool, if desired, make frosting crosses on the top with icing.

Icing
1 cup powdered sugar; 1 tablespoon water; 1/2 teaspoon vanilla; dash of salt.
Use a spoon to drizzle crosses on the top of the buns.

Potato Buns: To make potato buns, leave out the cinnamon and raisins.

****

Molasses Oatmeal Bread

Not only is this a rich, dark bread that makes terrific sandwiches and tasty toast, it's also high in fiber and low in refined sugar.

4 1/2 cups boiling water
2 cups dry oatmeal (either quick-cooking or old-fashioned; I like to use the old-fashioned because it gives the bread more texture)
1/2 cup shortening (I have also used Canola oil)
1/4 cup molasses
1/4 cup brown sugar
2 teaspoons salt
2 packages dry yeast (or 4 teaspoons bulk yeast)
10 to 12 cups flour

Measure the oatmeal into a mixing bowl and pour the boiling water over it. Let stand for a few minutes. Add shortening and stir to dissolve. Allow to cool to lukewarm. Stir in yeast. Add the molasses, brown sugar and salt. Stir in 2 cups of flour and beat until smooth. Add remaining flour. Knead until smooth. (Dough will be somewhat sticky.)

Put into a greased bowl and set in a warm place to rise for 45 minutes. Knead the dough for several minutes to remove air pockets. Shape into loaves. Makes 4 medium-sized loaves or 3 large loaves. You can also make round loaves and put them in pie plates. Let rise in a warm place for 45 minutes.

Bake at 350 degrees Fahrenheit for 45 minutes or until loaves are brown and sound hollow when tapped. Brush with shortening while the loaves still hot to help keep the crust soft. Let cool for a few minutes, and then remove the loaves from the pans.

****

Norma's Homemade Bread

My mother used to bake bread about once a week when I was growing up on our farm. Store-bought bread, she said, was "too fluffy" and "doesn't taste like anything." Here's the recipe for my mother's bread…

4 cups milk
1 stick butter
1/3 cup sugar
2 packages dry yeast (or 4 teaspoons bulk yeast)
1 1/2 teaspoons salt
8 to 10 cups of flour

Measure the milk into a saucepan, add the stick of butter and warm over medium heat until the butter melts.

Allow the hot milk mixture to cool to lukewarm. Stir in the yeast. Add the sugar and the salt. Add 2 cups of flour and beat until smooth. Add 1 more cup of flour and continue beating until smooth. Stir in the remaining flour. Knead until smooth (about five minutes).

Place in a large greased bowl and put in a warm place to rise for one hour. Punch down dough. Knead for another couple of minutes. Shape into loaves and put into greased loaf pans. Place in a warm place to rise for another 45 minutes.

Bake at 350 degrees Fahrenheit for 35 minutes or until loaves are light brown and sound hollow when tapped.

Brush the loaves with shortening after you take them out of the oven to keep the crust soft. Let cool 5 or 10 minutes and remove from pans.

Makes 3 large loaves or 4 medium loaves.

****

Extra-Nutty Nut 'n Raisin Bread

This nut bread goes great with a cup of coffee or tea or a glass of milk. The canola oil, walnuts, sunflower seeds and flaxseed make it a heart-healthy choice. Plus—it's an easy recipe! Instead of using whole flaxseed, you can increase the sunflower seeds to 1/2 cup if desired.

1/2 cup canola oil
1 1/2 cups sugar
3 eggs
1 1/2 cups of milk with 1/4 cup of lemon juice
1 1/2 teaspoons vanilla
4 cups flour
1 teaspoon baking powder
1 teaspoon baking soda
1/4 teaspoon salt
1 cup walnuts
1/4 cup sunflower seeds
1/4 cup whole flaxseed
1 cup raisins

Measure out the milk and add the 1/4 cup lemon juice. Set aside. Measure the remaining ingredients into a large mixing bowl. Add the milk. Using an electric mixer, stir on slow speed for 2 minutes and then on high speed for 2 to 3 minutes. Add chopped walnuts, sunflower seeds, flaxseed and raisins. Stir on low speed until nuts and raisins are blended in.

Divide the batter between 2 greased loaf pans. Bake at 350 degrees Fahrenheit for 60 minutes. Allow the nut bread to cool for 10 minutes before removing from the pans.

****

Nut Bread

When I was a kid growing up on our farm, my mother generally kept walnuts in the cupboard and used them frequently for baking, most often for making nut bread. Nowadays, we know that walnuts are heart-healthy. Back in the "good old days" we just thought walnuts were good. Who knew that they are good for you, too?

   1 cup brown sugar
   1 cup milk with 1 tablespoon of vinegar or lemon juice added to it
   1/4 cup Canola oil
   1 egg
   1/2 teaspoon salt
   1 teaspoon soda
   1 teaspoon vanilla
   2 1/2 cups flour
   1 cup chopped walnuts

Measure out the milk into a mixing bowl and add the vinegar or lemon juice. Let stand for a minute. Add the brown sugar and Canola oil and stir in. Beat in the egg. Add the salt, soda, vanilla and flour. Mix until thoroughly combined. Blend in the walnuts.

Spoon the batter into a greased loaf pan and bake at 350 degrees Fahrenheit for 60 to 70 minutes or until a toothpick comes out clean. Allow to cool before removing the walnut bread from the pan.

Date Nut Bread:
Add 1 cup of chopped dates to the batter.

Banana Nut Bread:
Mash 2 fully ripe bananas and add to the batter.

Raisin Nut Bread:
Add 1 cup of raisins to the batter.

****

Oatmeal-Apple-Raisin Muffins

These muffins are quick and easy to make for breakfast. I also make them for the coffee that's served after church on Sunday, too. The church is the same little white country church I attended as a child.

1 egg
1 cup buttermilk (or 1 cup of milk with 1 tablespoon of lemon juice added)
1 cup oatmeal (either quick-cooking or old-fashioned oatmeal; I like to use the old-fashioned oatmeal)
1/2 cup of brown sugar
1/2 cup cooking oil
2 cups flour
1 teaspoon baking powder
1/2 teaspoon salt
1/2 teaspoon baking soda
1/4 to 1/2 teaspoon cinnamon
1 medium-sized apple chopped
1/2 cup raisins
1/2 cup chopped walnuts (optional)

Pre-heat the oven to 375 degrees. Chop the apple into small pieces and put into a mixing bowl. Add the raisins. Measure out the remaining ingredients. Stir just until the dry ingredients are moistened. Grease muffin cups and fill to 2/3 full. Bake for 20 to 25 minutes or until golden brown. Allow to cool for 5 to 10 minutes, then remove from the muffin tins. Makes 2 dozen muffins.

Hint: Instead of greasing the muffin tins, use cupcake papers. I always do. That way I don't have to work so hard to scrub out my muffin tins!

Note: If you want bigger muffins, divide the batter into 12 muffin cups.

Extra note: Instead of chopped apple and raisins, you can use 1 1/2 to 2 cups of dried apricots cut into small pieces or 1 1/2 to 2 cups dried cranberries, if you like. Also add another quarter cup of milk to make up for the moisture in the apple pieces.

****

Potato Buns

This is the basic recipe for "Hot Cross Buns" but in case you missed the potato buns part of the recipe, here it is again!

2 packages dry yeast (or 4 teaspoons bulk yeast)
2 cups warm water
1 cup mashed potatoes
1/2 cup sugar
1/2 cup shortening
1 teaspoon salt
2 eggs
5 to 6 cups flour

Dissolve the yeast in warm water. Add the potatoes, sugar, shortening, salt, eggs and 2 cups of flour. Beat until smooth. Stir in remaining flour. If the dough seems much too sticky, add flour by the 1/2 cup until it's not quite as sticky.

Knead for about 5 minutes. (The dough will still be sticky and soft.) Place in a large, greased bowl and put in a warm place to rise for 1 hour.

Punch down dough. Shape the dough into 24 equal pieces. Place on a greased baking sheet. Let rise for 45 minutes.

Bake at 350 degrees Fahrenheit for 25 to 30 minutes or until golden brown.

****

Quick Bread Mix
(With recipes for pancakes, biscuits and muffins)

After my mom and dad retired from farming and moved to the house where I live now, I used to mix up this recipe for Mom so she would have it to make pancakes, biscuits or muffins.

10 cups flour
1/3 cup baking powder
1/4 cup sugar
1 tablespoon salt
2 cups vegetable shortening

Cut the shortening into the flour, baking powder, sugar and salt. Continue working the mixture with a fork or a pastry cutter until it resembles finely ground meal. Quick Bread Mix can be stored in an airtight container for 6 weeks.

Pancakes
    2 cups of Quick Bread Mix
    1 1/3 cup milk
    1 teaspoon vanilla
    2 tablespoons sugar
    2 eggs
If the pancake batter seems too thin, add a little more Quick Bread Mix. If the mixture seems too thick, add a little more milk.

Drop Biscuits
    2 cups of Quick Bread Mix
    1/2 cup milk
Mix thoroughly and then drop onto a greased baking sheet by spoonfuls. Bake at 350 degrees Fahrenheit for 15 to 20 minutes or until golden brown.

Muffins
    3 cups of Quick Bread Mix
    1 cup milk
    1 egg
    1/2 cup sugar

Blend all ingredients just until the Quick Bread Mix is moistened. Drop by spoonfuls into greased muffin tins or muffin tins lined with cupcake papers. Bake at 350 degrees Fahrenheit for 15 to 20 minutes or until golden brown. **Note:** to make blueberry muffins add 1 cup of blueberries; to make apple muffins, add 1 teaspoon cinnamon and 1 cup of chopped apples.

****

Refrigerator Muffins

If you like muffins for breakfast and snacks, this recipe makes enough batter for lots of muffins. You can mix the batter up, refrigerate it and then bake muffins as you need them. One batch of batter will make about six dozen muffins (more or less), depending on the size of the muffin tins.

2 cups hot water
1 cup of wheat germ
1 cup of Canola oil (or another cooking oil)
3 cups sugar
4 eggs
4 cups of buttermilk (or milk with 4 tablespoons of vinegar or lemon juice)
9 cups flour
5 teaspoons soda
2 teaspoons salt
6 cups bran flake cereal (raisin bran works well)

Measure the wheat germ into a mixing bowl. Pour the hot water over the wheat germ. Let sit for a few minutes. Measure the Canola oil into the mixing bowl. Add the sugar. Beat in the eggs. Stir in the buttermilk or sour milk. Add the flour, soda and salt and stir together until thoroughly combined. Fold in the bran cereal until moistened.

Fill muffin cups lined with cupcake papers three-quarters full and bake at 350 degrees Fahrenheit for 20 to 25 minutes or until golden brown.

Store remaining batter in the refrigerator until you are ready to bake more muffins.

****

Scones

My mother enjoyed these biscuits with a cup of coffee. They are especially good if you make them with dried cranberries.

4 cups flour
1/2 cup butter
1/2 teaspoon salt
1 teaspoon baking powder
1/2 cup sugar
1/2 cup raisins or dried cranberries (optional)
2 eggs
1 cup milk

Measure flour into a mixing bowl. Cut in the butter with a fork. Add the salt, sugar, and raisins (or cranberries) (if desired).

Measure the milk into a small mixing bowl. Beat the eggs into the milk. Pour the milk and egg mixture over the dry ingredients. Stir until the well mixed in. Knead for a minute or two until dough is moist.

Turn dough onto a well-floured surface. Roll out dough to about 3/4 inch thick. Use a biscuit cutter to cut out the scones.

Arrange on an ungreased cookie sheet and bake at 350 degrees Fahrenheit for 25 or 30 minutes until golden brown. Remove from cookie sheet. Allow to cool before serving.

Makes 12 to 18 scones, depending on the size of the biscuit cutter.

****

Quick & Easy Sour Cream Crescent Rolls

If you want to serve fresh homemade crescent rolls for a special dinner or family get-together, this recipe takes about 2 hours from start to finish. And they're delicious. If I do say so myself. And I think I just did.

2 packages of dry yeast (or 4 teaspoons bulk yeast)
1 cup warm water
1 cup buttermilk (or 1 cup milk with 1 tablespoon of lemon juice added)
1/2 cup sour cream
1 stick butter softened
1/3 cup sugar
1 teaspoon salt
6 to 7 cups flour

Dissolve the yeast in the warm water. Let sit for a few minutes. Add buttermilk, sour cream, butter, sugar, salt and 2 cups of flour. Use an electric mixer or a wire whisk and blend for several minutes. Add the remaining flour. Knead for 5 minutes. Let the dough rest for 20 minutes.

To make the crescent rolls: divide the dough in half. Roll each half into a 12-inch circle (mine usually ends up being more of rectangle than a circle, but it works, so who cares?). Spread soft butter onto the circle of dough. Cut the circle in half. Cut each half into quarters. Then cut each quarter into three pieces (as if you are cutting a pie).

Roll up each piece of dough, beginning with the wide end. Place on a greased cookie sheet with the "point" underneath. Let rise in a warm place for 45 minutes before baking.

Bake at 350 degrees Fahrenheit for 20 to 25 minutes or until golden brown. Allow to cool for 10 minutes and then remove from the cookie sheet.

This recipe makes 2 dozen crescent rolls. Total time (including time to bake) is about 2 hours.

****

Cinnamon Tea Ring

A fancy version of Cinnamon Rolls—and easy, too! This pastry looks like you spent hours slaving over the dough. In reality, it takes 2 hours from start to finish because it is basically my cinnamon roll recipe (well, maybe it takes a bit more than 2 hours when you add the frosting glaze). I have made this for the breakfast after the Sunday school Christmas program and for coffee after church on Sundays and there usually is not much left to take home.

> **2 cups warm water**
> **2 packages of dry yeast (or 4 teaspoons bulk yeast)**
> **1/2 cup sugar**
> **1 teaspoon salt**
> **1/2 cup cooking oil (I like to use Canola oil)**
> **2 eggs**
> **6 to 7 cups of flour**
> **1 cup chopped walnuts (optional)**

To decorate:
> **walnuts**
> **candied cherries**

Frosting Glaze:
> **3 to 4 cups of powdered sugar**
> **1 teaspoon of vanilla**
> **a pinch of salt**

Add water or milk by the tablespoon until the glaze will dribble off a spoon.

****

Measure warm water into a large mixing bowl and dissolve yeast in warm water. Let sit for a few minutes. Stir in sugar, salt, cooking oil. Beat in eggs. Beat in 2 to 3 cups of flour. Stir in remaining flour. Knead on a floured surface for about five minutes. If dough is too sticky, knead in a little more flour, a quarter cup at a time.

Let the dough rest for 20 minutes. Then knead the dough again for a few minutes.

Roll out dough into a rectangle approximately 24 inches long by about 16 inches wide. Spread with soft butter. Sprinkle with sugar and cinnamon. (1 cup of sugar and 1 teaspoon of cinnamon mixed together). Beginning on the wide side, roll up dough. When the dough is rolled, be sure the seam is on the bottom. Grasp dough on each end and pull gently to stretch the dough another couple of inches. Cut the roll of dough in half. Grease two cookie sheets.

Take each end of one roll and put them together on the cookie sheet to form a circle. Use a scissors to cut about a third to a half the way through the dough at two-inch intervals all around the circle. Gently turn the dough outward. That is, grasp the dough and turn it on its side so that the cuts are on the outside instead of on the top. Repeat with the other roll.

Set in a warm place to rise for 45 minutes.

Bake at 350 degrees Fahrenheit for 25 to 35 minutes.

Allow the tea rings to cool completely and then remove them from the cookie sheets. Place on a platter or a serving plate.

Frost with powder sugar glaze. Use a spoon to drizzle the glaze over the tea rings. Decorate with walnuts and/or candied cherries before the glaze has a chance to set.

Cut into slices to serve.

****

Whole Wheat Batter Bread

From start to finish, this bread takes about an hour and a half. And no kneading!

1 cup whole wheat flour
4 cups white flour
1/4 cup wheat germ
2 pkgs. dry yeast (or 4 teaspoons bulk yeast)
1 cup warm milk
2 1/4 cups warm water
1 tablespoon sugar
1 teaspoon salt
1/4 teaspoon baking powder

Measure 1 cup of whole-wheat flour, 1 cup white flour, wheat germ, yeast, sugar, salt and baking soda into a large mixing bowl.

Stir in warm milk and water. Using an electric mixer (preferably one with dough hooks!), mix on low speed for a minute and then on high speed for a couple of minutes. Add the 3 remaining cups of white flour. Continue mixing until the flour is thoroughly combined. Dough will be stiff and very sticky.

Grease 2 loaf pans. Divide the dough equally between the 2 pans. Put in a warm place to rise for 30 minutes.

Bake at 375 for 30 to 35 minutes until golden brown.

Immediately brush tops with shortening. Allow the bread to cool for about 10 minutes and then remove the loaves from the pans. Allow bread to cool completely before cutting.

Note: the bread will fall a little as it is baking so that you end up a "dip" in the loaves.

****

Whole Wheat Butter Biscuits

These biscuits go well with soup or stew. They also are delicious with butter and homemade jelly or jam!

1 stick of butter (1/2 cup)
2 cups white flour
1 cup whole wheat flour
3 teaspoons sugar
1/2 teaspoon salt
3 teaspoons baking powder
1 cup milk

Cut the butter into the flour with a fork until it resembles coarsely ground meal. Turn onto to a lightly floured surface and knead for a minute or two.

Roll out the dough a half inch thick and cut out the biscuits with a round donut cutter or other biscuit cutter. Place biscuits on an ungreased baking sheet and bake at 400 degrees for 15 minutes.

This recipe makes about a dozen biscuits, depending on the size of the biscuit cutter you use.

****

Whole Wheat Oatmeal Waffles

When I was a kid growing up on our dairy farm, one of my favorite breakfasts was waffles served with syrup and a scoop of ice cream. It was the only time my mother let me eat ice cream for breakfast. Sometimes during the winter, I make these for supper and serve with strawberries I have taken out of the freezer. Strawberries on a cold January night are good for the soul.

2 cups milk
2 eggs
1/2 cup Canola oil (or another vegetable oil)
1/2 cup dry oatmeal
1 cup whole wheat flour
1 cup white flour
2 tablespoons sugar
1/2 teaspoon salt
1/2 teaspoon baking soda
1/2 teaspoon baking powder
1 teaspoon vanilla

Measure the milk into a mixing bowl. Add the dry oatmeal. Let sit for 5 to 10 minutes. Stir in the other ingredients. Mix thoroughly.

If the batter seems too thick, add more milk by the tablespoon. If the batter seems too thin, add more flour by the tablespoon. Bake according to the directions for your waffle iron.

Serve with syrup, fresh fruit, canned peach slices, ice cream, whipped cream—whatever sounds good to you.

****

Whole Wheat Oatmeal Bread

This recipe makes four loaves of bread. It's a good way to add fiber to your diet. And as is the case with any bread that you bake, it makes the house smell really good.

4 cups of warm water
2 packages of dry yeast (or 4 teaspoons of bulk yeast)
1/2 cup of sugar
1/2 cup Canola oil (or another vegetable oil)
2 teaspoons salt
1/2 cup dry oatmeal
4 cups of whole wheat flour
4 to 6 cups of white flour

Measure the water into a large mixing bowl. Stir in the yeast and dry oatmeal and let stand for a few minutes. Stir in the sugar and salt and the Canola oil. Add a cup of whole wheat flour and beat until smooth. Add another cup of whole wheat flour and beat until smooth. Add the last 2 cups of whole wheat flour and beat until smooth. Gradually stir in 3 to 4 cups of white flour until the dough is stiff enough to knead. Add 1 to 2 cups more of white flour while kneading. You will know you have added enough white flour when the dough is soft but not especially sticky.

Grease a large bowl. Put the dough into the bowl, cover with a towel and put the bowl into a warm place. Let the dough rise for 45 minutes.

Knead the dough for a couple of minutes. Divide into 4 loaves and put into greased loaf pans. To make round loaves: shape the dough into a round and place in a pie plate.

Put the pans into a warm place and let rise for another 45 minutes.

Bake at 350 degrees Fahrenheit for 30 to 35 minutes (until the loaves are golden brown). Brush with shortening when the loaves come out of the oven.

Allow to the bread to cool for 10 minutes before removing the loaves from the pans.

****

Whole Wheat Buttermilk Bread
(Quick Recipe)

This recipe skips the step of letting the bread dough rise in a bowl for an hour.

2 packages of dry yeast (or 4 teaspoons of bulk yeast)
3/4 cup warm water
1 1/4 cups buttermilk (or 1 1/8 cups milk with 2 tablespoons lemon juice)
1/4 cup butter (softened) (or you can use 1/4 canola oil)
2 eggs
3 tablespoons sugar
1/2 teaspoon salt
1 cup whole wheat flour
4 cups white flour

Dissolve the yeast in the warm water. Add buttermilk, butter, eggs, sugar, salt and 1 cup of whole wheat flour. Beat until smooth. Stir in the remaining flour.

Turn onto a floured surface and knead for 5 minutes. Allow dough to rest for 20 minutes. Knead for 1 or 2 minutes. Shape into loaves and put the loaves in greased loaf pans (makes 2 loaves). Put in a warm place and let the loaves rise for 1 hour.

Bake at 350 degrees Fahrenheit for 35 to 40 minutes or until loaves sound hollow when tapped. Brush with shortening to keep the crust soft.

Allow to cool for 5 to 10 minutes, and then turn loaves out of the pans to finish cooling.

****

Cakes, Pies
&
Desserts

Apple Cake

Note: when I use apples in a cake or pie recipe, I don't peel them. Apple peeling contains pectin, which is one of the foods that help lower cholesterol in your bloodstream. Plus, the peeling adds a bit of color to the cake.

1 1/2 cups sugar
1/2 cup shortening
1 egg
1 cup of buttermilk (or 1 cup sweet milk to which you have added 1 tablespoon of vinegar or lemon juice)
1 teaspoon baking soda
1/4 teaspoon salt
2 cups flour
2 cups of unpeeled apples cut into small pieces

<u>**Topping:**</u>
1/2 cup brown sugar
1/2 teaspoon cinnamon
1/2 cup chopped walnuts

Measure the sugar and shortening into a mixing bowl. Cream together. Beat in the egg. Add the buttermilk/sour milk, baking soda, salt and flour. Beat until smooth. Stir in the apple pieces. Spoon the batter into a greased 9x13 pan. Measure the brown sugar, cinnamon and chopped nuts into a small mixing bowl. Stir until thoroughly combined. Sprinkle on top of cake batter.

Bake at 350 degrees Fahrenheit for 40 to 45 minutes or until the top of the cake springs back when you tap it with your finger. Allow to cool before cutting.

****

Apple Crisp

There's nothing like the smell of Apple Crisp baking on a cool fall day or on a blustery Sunday afternoon in February.

Crust:
   4 cups flour
   1 cup white sugar
   1 cup brown sugar
   1 stick butter
   1/2 cup shortening
   1/2 teaspoon salt

Filling:
   6 to 8 cups of apples cut into small pieces
   1 to 1 1/2 cups of sugar (use 1 1/2 if the apples are very tart) (if the apples are sweet, you may not need to use any sugar at all)
   1/2 cup flour
   1 teaspoon cinnamon

Note: Instead of butter and shortening, I have also made this recipe with 1 cup Canola oil (or use another vegetable oil, if you prefer)

Measure the flour, sugar, salt and butter and shortening into a mixing bowl. Use a fork to mix thoroughly (as you would if you were cutting shortening into flour to make pie crust).

Spoon half of the crust mixture into a 9x13 pan. Pat down with your fingers or the back of a spoon. Bake at 350 degrees Fahrenheit for 10 minutes.

Cut up the apples and put them into a large mixing bowl. Sprinkle the flour, sugar and cinnamon over the apples. Mix thoroughly.

When the crust comes out of the oven, spoon the apple mixture over the hot crust. Sprinkle the remaining crust mixture over the apples.

Bake for 45 to 50 minutes longer.

Allow to cool before cutting. Serve with whipped cream or ice cream if desired.

* * * * * * * * * * * * * * * * * * * *

Apple Dumplings

An elegant little pastry treat, apple dumplings are truly one of my favorites. My mother liked these Apple Dumplings, too. And they are among my husband's favorites.

Pastry:
   2/3 cup shortening
   2 cups flour
   1/2 teaspoon salt
   4 to 5 tablespoons of cold water

Measure shortening, flour and salt into a mixing bowl. Mix together with a fork. Gradually stir in the water to form the dough. Set aside.

Apples:
Core 6 baking apples but do not peel. Sprinkle cinnamon in the middle, if desired. Set aside.

Putting the Apple Dumplings Together:

Use 2/3 of the dough and roll into a square about 14 inches across. Cut the square into four pieces. Roll the remaining dough into a rectangle 14 inches by 7 inches and cut into two squares.

Place one apple in the center of one piece of dough. Use the tip of your finger to moisten edges of dough with water. Pull the four corners of the dough up over the top of the apple and seal. Tuck in the rest of the dough on the sides around the apple and press to seal. (It's sort of like wrapping a Christmas present.) Repeat with the rest of the apples and the dough. Place the apples in an oblong baking dish.

Sauce:
   1 cup brown sugar
   2 cups of water

Heat the brown sugar and water to boiling in a saucepan and then carefully pour the syrup around the apples. Bake at 350 degrees Fahrenheit for 50 to 60 minutes or until the apples are tender and the crust is golden brown. While the dumplings are baking, occasionally spoon the syrup over the dumplings (3 or 4 times during the baking process) (a turkey baster works well).

Serve warm or cold with whipped cream or vanilla ice cream.

Note: I have also used fresh peaches with this recipe and made peach dumplings. Yum!

* * * * * * * * * * * * * * * * * * * *

Apple Upside-Down Dessert

My husband says that this recipe is a "keeper." It is especially good served warm with vanilla ice cream or frozen Cool Whip (or another similar topping).

6 to 8 apples
1 cup sugar
1/4 cup Canola oil (or another vegetable oil)
1 cup milk
2 cups flour
1/2 teaspoon salt
1 teaspoon vanilla
1 cup very hot water (to pour over the cake)

Topping:
1 cup sugar
1/4 cup flour
1 teaspoon cinnamon

Wash the apples, pat dry and cut into slices. (Do not peel the apples.) Arrange the apple slices to cover the bottom of a greased 9x13 pan.

Measure the sugar, cooking oil, milk, flour, salt and vanilla into a mixing bowl and, using an electric mixer, beat on low speed for a minute, scraping the bowl as you go. Then beat on high speed for a couple of minutes. Spoon the batter over the apples.

Measure the sugar, flour and cinnamon into a mixing bowl and stir until thoroughly combined. Sprinkle over the batter. Pour one cup of hot water over the top of the mixture in the pan.

Bake at 350 degrees Fahrenheit for 60 minutes.

****

Baked Oatmeal Supreme

Made with oatmeal, raisins, walnuts and milk, Baked Oatmeal Supreme is a heart-healthy—and delicious!—way to start your day (makes an excellent in between meals snack, too). If your children or grandchildren or spouse do not like oatmeal for breakfast, they might think this is tasty. It's worth a try, anyway.

2 cups dry oatmeal (I like to use old-fashioned oatmeal)
1/4 to 1/2 cup brown sugar (1/2 cup makes it very sweet)
1 1/2 cups milk
2 eggs
1 teaspoon baking powder
1/4 to 1/2 teaspoon salt
1/2 teaspoon cinnamon
1/2 cup chopped walnuts (or slivered almonds)
1/2 cup raisins (or dried cranberries)

Measure all ingredients into a mixing bowl. Use a fork to mix together thoroughly. Pour into a greased 8x8 casserole dish. Bake for 40 to 45 minutes at 350 degrees Fahrenheit. Serve with milk if desired. This also is good cold as an in-between meal snack or as a dessert.

****

Butterscotch Brownies

These brownies are baked in an 8x8-inch pan. They are quite tasty—and since it's a small pan, I'm not tempted to eat so many!

1/4 cup canola oil (or another vegetable oil)
1 cup packed brown sugar
1 egg
1 teaspoon of vanilla
1/2 teaspoon salt
3/4 cup flour
1 cup chopped walnuts or walnuts cut into pieces

Measure the canola oil, brown sugar, egg, vanilla and salt into a mixing bowl. Beat with a spoon or electric mixer until smooth. Stir in the flour and walnuts until thoroughly combined. Spread into a greased 8x8 pan.

Bake for about 25 minutes at 350 degrees Fahrenheit or until the brownies are firm when tapped with your forefinger. Allow to cool before cutting.

****

Butter Cake
(With Whipped Cream Cherry or Blueberry Frosting)

This "plain yellow" cake can be frosted or served plain and used as strawberry shortcake served with sweetened strawberries and whipped cream. Instead of butter, you can also make this cake with 2/3 cup of Canola oil or another cooking oil.

2 cups flour
1 1/2 cups sugar
3 teaspoons baking powder
1/2 teaspoon salt
1/2 cup butter (softened)
1 cup milk
1 teaspoon vanilla
3 eggs

Measure the flour, sugar, baking powder, salt, butter, milk, vanilla and eggs into a mixing bowl. Use an electric mixer and beat on slow speed for 1 minute, scraping the bowl as you go. Then beat on high speed for 2 or 3 minutes.

Bake in a greased 9x13 pan at 350 degrees Fahrenheit for 35 or 40 minutes until the top springs back when tapped with your finger. Allow to cool before frosting.

****

Whipped Cream Cherry or Blueberry Frosting

1 1/2 cups whipping cream
1/4 to 1/2 cup white sugar or powdered sugar (depending on how sweet you want it)
1 can of cherry or blueberry pie filling

Measure cream into a medium sized mixing bowl. Whip at high speed with an electric mixer until the cream begins to thicken. Add sugar gradually while continuing to whip. Finish whipping the cream until it reaches the desired consistency (thick and forms peaks when you lift out the beaters). Carefully fold in the cherry or blueberry pie filling.

Spread over cake. Refrigerate an hour or two before serving. Keep remaining cake refrigerated.

****

Caramel Apple Dessert

The preparation time for this recipe is somewhat time-consuming (cutting up the apples and unwrapping and cutting up the caramel candies), but the result is worth it! Once the apples and caramels are ready, the rest of the recipe goes quickly.

1 cup brown sugar
2/3 cup Canola oil (or other cooking oil)
2 cups flour
1 1/2 cups quick-cooking oatmeal
1/2 teaspoon salt
1/2 teaspoon baking soda
4 cups of chopped apples
1/4 cup flour
16 ounces of caramel candies

Unwrap the caramel candies and cut each one into four pieces and set aside. Cut the apples into small pieces and set aside in a mixing bowl.

Measure the brown sugar, cooking oil, flour, oatmeal, salt and baking soda into a medium-sized mixing bowl and stir with a fork until well combined. Remove 1 1/2 cups and set aside. Press the remaining flour and oatmeal mixture into an ungreased 9x13 pan.

Mix 1/4 cup of flour with the apples and sprinkle over the crust in the pan. Sprinkle the caramel candy pieces over the apples. Sprinkle the reserved 1 1/2 cups of crust mixture over the caramel and apples. Bake at 375 degrees Fahrenheit for 40 to 45 minutes.

****

Cheesecake Parfait
("Died and Gone to Heaven" Good!)

This recipe is not especially heart-healthy—or any kind of healthy. But, if you are looking for a sumptuous dessert (maybe to serve for a special occasion) that is "Died and Gone to Heaven" good, this is it.

Lower-Fat Alternative: you can make a lower-fat version of this recipe using low-fat cream cheese, low-fat topping, and use skim milk with the instant pudding.

Bottom layer:
    2 sticks butter
    3 cups flour
    1 cup chopped walnuts

Mix the butter, flour and walnuts as you would for pie crust. Pat into an ungreased 9x13 pan and bake at 350 degrees Fahrenheit for 25 to 30 minutes. Allow to cool.

Second layer:
    2 eight-ounce packages of cream cheese (softened)
    2 cups of powdered sugar
    2 cups of Cool Whip (or another similar topping)

Measure into a mixing bowl and whip at high speed until smooth. Spread over the first layer.

Third layer:
    2 three-ounce packages of instant pudding (any flavor—chocolate, lemon, butterscotch, vanilla, pistachio— whatever you like)
    3 cups of milk

Pour instant pudding into a mixing bowl, add the milk, and whip at high speed for several minutes until thick. Spread over the cream cheese layer.

Fourth layer:
Spread on enough Cool Whip (or another topping) to cover the pudding. Sprinkle with chopped nuts and coconut.

Chill the dessert in the refrigerator for at least an hour before serving.

****

Cherry (or Blueberry) Blintzes

Making the crepes for this recipe is a little time-consuming. But the Blintzes are worth it!

Crepes:
  1 1/2 cups flour
  2 tablespoons sugar
  1/2 teaspoon baking powder
  1/4 teaspoon salt
  2 cups milk
  2 eggs
  1/2 teaspoon vanilla

Measure all ingredients into a mixing bowl. Use an electric mixer or a rotary beater to beat until smooth.

Use a pastry brush to coat the bottom of a cast iron or Teflon-coated 8-inch frying pan. Heat the pan for a minute or so on medium to medium-high heat.

Pour 1/4 cup of the batter into the skillet, and rotate the skillet to spread out the batter across the bottom. Cook until light brown, turn and cook until light brown on the other side. Stack crepes on a plate. Makes about a dozen crepes. Brush pan with shortening before cooking each crepe.

Filling:
  1 cup cottage cheese
  1/2 cup sour cream
  2 tablespoons sugar
  1 teaspoon lemon juice
  1 teaspoon vanilla
  1 can of cherry or blueberry pie filling

Measure the cottage cheese, sour cream, sugar, lemon juice and vanilla into a bowl and stir until thoroughly combined. Put 1 to 2 tablespoons of filling on the middle of a crepe. Fold over the sides of the crepe and then roll up. Brush the skillet with shortening again. Place crepes seam side down in the skillet. Cook over medium heat until heated through.

Serve warm with a couple of tablespoons of cherry (or blueberry) pie filling on top of each crepe and a dollop of whipped cream, if desired.

****

Chocolate Chip Peanut Butter Bars

Another one of my husband's favorites. Mine, too.

1/2 cup butter (softened)
1/2 cup shortening
1 cup granulated sugar
1 cup brown sugar
1 cup peanut butter
2 eggs
1 teaspoon vanilla
3 cups flour
1 teaspoon baking soda
1/2 teaspoon salt
1 package (11-12 ounces) chocolate chips

Measure the butter, shortening, white sugar, brown sugar and peanut butter into a large mixing bowl and mix until well combined. Beat in the eggs and the vanilla. Stir in the flour, baking powder and salt. Stir in the chocolate chips. Dough will be fairly stiff.

Grease a 9x13 inch pan and drop the dough into the pan by large spoonfuls. Use the back of the spoon to smooth out the dough. Bake at 350 degrees Fahrenheit for 30 to 35 minutes (or until the center feels firm when you touch it lightly).

Allow to cool before cutting.

✳✳✳✳✳✳✳✳✳✳✳✳✳✳✳✳✳✳✳✳

Chocolate Éclairs
(Easy Recipe!)

Chocolate Éclairs are an elegant dessert —and they are very easy to make. My husband likes to take them to eat for dessert after lunch at work. He also likes to eat them for breakfast.

1 1/2 cups water
1/2 cup butter
1 1/2 cups flour
5 eggs
1 package of regular instant pudding (or sugar-free, if desired) (any flavor you like; vanilla, chocolate, lemon. . .) (note: use 2 packages of instant pudding if you want the Éclairs heaped with pudding.)
Chocolate Icing (recipe below)

Measure the water and butter into a medium sized saucepan. Bring the water and butter to a full rolling boil. Remove pan from the burner. Stir in the flour until thoroughly mixed in. Add the eggs to the mixture in the pan. Stir until the eggs are thoroughly mixed in and the dough becomes smooth. A fork works well to beat in the eggs.

To form the Éclairs, measure out the dough by scant half-cups and shape into oblong shapes on an ungreased baking sheet. (Éclairs will be about four inches long by three inches wide.) (Recipe makes approximately one dozen Éclairs.) Bake at 375 degrees Fahrenheit for 40 minutes.

Allow the Éclairs to cool completely. Remove from the baking sheet and place on a large plate.

Mix the pudding according to package directions. When the pudding is set, cut off the tops of the Éclairs and fill with pudding. Replace tops.

Chocolate Icing:
1 tablespoon of butter
3 teaspoons cocoa
1 cup powdered sugar
1 to 2 tablespoons water

Melt butter. Mix in the cocoa. Add the powdered sugar and 1 to 2 tablespoons water. Stir until smooth. If you use 2 tablespoons of water and the icing is too thin, add powdered sugar by the tablespoon until the icing reaches the desired consistency.

Drizzle icing over the Éclairs. (Keep remaining Éclairs refrigerated.)

****

Chocolate Cherry Cake

The marshmallows float to the top and the cherries sink to the bottom.

**3 cups flour
2 teaspoons baking soda
1 teaspoon salt
1/2 cup cocoa
2 cups sugar
1 teaspoon vanilla
2 tablespoons vinegar
2/3 cup cooking oil
2 cups cold water
3 cups miniature marshmallows
21 oz. can cherry pie filling**

Measure the flour, baking soda, salt, cocoa, sugar, vanilla, vinegar, cooking oil and water into a mixing bowl and blend with an electric mixer on low speed for 1 to 2 minutes and on high speed for 3 minutes.

Grease a 9x13 cake pan. Spread the marshmallows in the bottom of the pan. Pour the cake batter over the marshmallows. Drop the pie filling by spoonfuls at even intervals on the batter.

Bake at 350 degrees Fahrenheit for 45 to 50 minutes.

Frost cake if desired, or serve with whipped cream or ice cream.

****

Chocolate Raspberry Layer Cake

My husband loves raspberries, and this is one of his favorite desserts. I often make it as a birthday cake for him. The recipe (like the parfait dessert) can in no way, shape or form be considered a "heart healthy" recipe. But it *is* delicious! Also good with cherry pie filling instead of raspberry.

3 cups flour
1 teaspoon baking soda
1 teaspoon baking powder
1 teaspoon salt
1/2 cup cocoa
2 cups sugar
1 teaspoon vanilla
2 tablespoons vinegar
2/3 cup cooking oil
2 cups cold water
1 can of raspberry pie filling (or cherry pie filling)
Frosting (recipe included below)

Measure the flour, baking soda, salt, cocoa, sugar, vanilla, vinegar, cooking oil and water into a mixing bowl and blend with an electric mixer on low speed for 1 to 2 minutes and on high speed for 3 minutes. Divide the batter between 2 greased and floured layer cake pans. Bake at 350 degrees Fahrenheit for 35 to 40 minutes or until cake is done and leaves no impression when patted lightly with your finger. Allow layers to cool completely. Remove first layer from the pan and place on a cake plate. Whip up the frosting.

Frosting:
3/4 cup shortening
3/4 cup butter
3/4 cup milk
1 1/2 cups of white sugar or brown sugar (the brown sugar makes a sweeter frosting)
2 teaspoons vanilla
1/2 cup plus two tablespoons flour

Warm the shortening, butter and milk in the microwave slightly to take off the chill— or else allow the ingredients to warm to room temperature. Put all ingredients into a large mixing bowl. Using an electric mixer, whip at high speed for five minutes, scraping the sides of the bowl occasionally with a plastic or rubber scraper.

Frost the bottom layer and spread half the can of raspberry pie filling on top of the frosting. Remove the other layer from the pan and place on top of the first layer. Use the remaining frosting to frost the sides and top of the cake. Spread the remaining raspberry pie filling on top of the cake.

****

Cinnamon-Apple Coffee Cake

Another recipe for Autumn when the apples are plentiful. You can also use frozen apple slices.

3 cups flour
1 cup sugar
4 teaspoons baking powder
1 teaspoon salt
1/2 cup cooking oil
1 cup of milk
2 eggs
1 teaspoon cinnamon
2 to 3 apples cut up in small pieces

Filling:
2/3 cup brown sugar
1 teaspoon cinnamon
1/2 to 2/3 cup chopped walnuts (optional)
1/2 to 2/3 cup coconut (optional)
1/4 cup soft butter

Measure all ingredients except the apples and the filling into a mixing bowl and stir by hand or with an electric mixer for several minutes. Stir in apples. Grease a 9x13 pan. Put one half of the batter into the pan. Mix up the filling. Drop by spoonfuls on top of the batter in the pan. Add the remaining batter.

Bake at 350 degrees Fahrenheit for 35 to 40 minutes. Allow to cool before cutting.

****

Cinnamon Coffee Cake

My mother loved cinnamon. I do, too, although I have to be careful when the ragweed is pollinating because I can get a "cross reactivity" reaction from cinnamon. Cinnamon Coffee Cake makes a nice breakfast treat for Sunday mornings—or any other time you're in the mood for a taste of cinnamon.

2 cups flour
1/2 teaspoon baking soda
1 teaspoon baking powder
1/2 teaspoon of salt
1/4 cup Canola oil
1 cup sugar
1 cup buttermilk (or add 1 tablespoon of lemon juice to 1 cup of milk)
2 eggs
1 teaspoon vanilla
1 tablespoon cinnamon (use less if you don't want as strong a cinnamon taste)

Measure the sugar, Canola oil, sour milk and eggs in a mixing bowl. Beat until smooth with an electric mixer. Add vanilla and cinnamon. Mix in the flour, baking soda, baking powder and salt.

Bake in a greased loaf pan at 350 degrees Fahrenheit for 40 minutes or until the top springs back when touched lightly with your finger. Allow to cool before removing from the pan.

****

Cinnamon Roll Coffee Cake

This recipe is baked in an angel food cake pan. Make and serve for a special occasion —or "just because" when you want a treat.

2 cups warm water
4 teaspoons of bulk yeast (or two packages of yeast)
1/2 cup sugar
1 teaspoon salt
1/2 cup canola oil (or other cooking oil)
2 eggs
5 to 6 cups of flour (I like to use 1 or 2 cups of whole wheat flour and the rest white flour).
6 tablespoons butter (melted)
1 cup of sugar
2 to 3 teaspoons cinnamon

Dissolve the yeast in the warm water. Let stand for a couple of minutes. Stir in sugar, salt and cooking oil. Beat in eggs. Add 1 cup of flour and stir until smooth. Add 2 more cups of flour and stir until smooth. Add remaining flour—enough to make a dough that is a little sticky.

Let the dough rest for 20 minutes.

While the dough is resting, grease the angel food cake pan. Mix up the sugar and cinnamon. Melt the butter. Tear off chunks of dough the size of a small egg. Roll the dough between your palms to make it smooth. Roll in the melted butter. Roll in the cinnamon and sugar. Place in the bottom of the angel food cake pan. Don't fit the dough balls into the pan too tightly. They need room to rise. Line the bottom of the pan, then add more layers until the dough is all used.

Allow to rise in a warm place for 45 minutes. Bake in a 350 degree Fahrenheit oven for 40 minutes or until golden brown.

Let cool for 10 to 15 minutes. Turn the coffee cake out onto a large cake plate.

To serve, use a fork to separate pieces of the coffee cake.

****

Cream Cheese Mincemeat Pie

If you like mincemeat, you might like this pie, too. I made it for a pie social for church and was asked for the recipe because it was "unusual." You can use the recipe for no-roll pie crust for the bottom curst. I have also used green tomato mincemeat in this recipe.

bottom pie crust for a 9 or 10 inch pie plate
3 cups mincemeat
8 ounces of cream cheese (softened)
1/2 cup sugar
1 egg
1 tablespoon lemon juice

Make the pie crust and line the pie plate with the crust. Spoon the mincemeat on top of the pie crust. Bake at 350 degrees Fahrenheit for 20 to 25 minutes. Using an electric mixer, whip the softened cream cheese, sugar, the egg and the lemon juice until smooth. Pour on top of the mincemeat and bake for another 25 to 30 minutes or until set. Allow to cool before cutting.

****

No-Roll Pie Crust

1 1/2 cups flour
1/2 teaspoon salt
1 teaspoons sugar
1/3 cup cooking oil (I like to use Canola oil)
4 tablespoons water or milk

Measure all ingredients into a medium mixing bowl. Stir with a fork until thoroughly combined. Roll out and line the pie plate.

****

Cream Puffs

When I was a kid, cream puffs were a "quick to fix" dessert if we were temporarily out of pie or cake or cookies. Serve filled with whipped cream or your favorite kind of ice cream or your favorite pudding.

1 cup water
1/2 cup butter
1 cup flour
4 eggs

Measure the water into a medium sized saucepan. Add the stick of butter. Use a spoon to cut the stick of butter into pieces (it melts faster that way). Turn the burner on medium-high and bring to a full rolling boil. Stir in the flour. Take the pan off the burner. Beat in the eggs all at once.

Drop by 1/4 cups or 1/2 cups onto an ungreased baking sheet. (If you want smaller cream puffs, use 1/4 dough for each.) Bake at 375 degrees for 35 to 40 minutes. Remove from the baking sheet. Allow to cool.

To serve, cut off the tops, fill with whipped cream, ice cream or pudding.

Makes 6 to 12 cream puffs, depending on if you use 1/4 or 1/2 cup of dough for each one.

$$*******************$$

Double-Fudge Parfait

This "simply" elegant dessert will make your family (and guests) think you slaved for hours.

1 package of chocolate instant pudding mix
1 package of coconut
1 package of chocolate chips (milk chocolate or semi-sweet)
1 jar of dry-roasted peanuts
4 wine glasses or stemmed water glasses
fresh strawberries, raspberries or kiwi fruit

Prepare the pudding mix according to package directions.

Place several spoonfuls of pudding in the bottom of the glasses, then alternate layers of several tablespoons of coconut, chocolate chips and dry-roasted peanuts with layers of pudding. Garnish with fresh strawberries, raspberries or sliced kiwi if desired. You can also layer the fruit, if you want, along with the other ingredients. Use either milk chocolate or semi-sweet chocolate chips according to what you like best.

****

Easy Blueberry (or Cherry) Cheesecake Recipe

Cheesecake has always been one of my favorites! In fact, anything with cream cheese …

Crust:
2 packages of graham crackers (18 "cracker sheets")
1/2 cup (1 stick) butter

Crush the graham crackers (I put 4 or 5 "cracker sheets" at a time into a sturdy plastic freezer bag and crush them with a rolling pin). Put cracker crumbs into a medium-sized bowl and pour melted butter/margarine over the crumbs. Mix thoroughly. Press into a 9x13 ungreased pan.

Batter:
8 ounces of cream cheese (softened)
1 egg
1 can (14 ounces) sweetened, condensed milk
3 tablespoons lemon juice
1 can (21 ounces) of blueberry or cherry pie filling

Use an electric mixer to beat the cream cheese and sweetened condensed milk until smooth (a minute or two). Add the lemon juice and egg and beat on high speed for another minute.

Pour the batter over the graham cracker crust. Drop the canned pie filling into the batter by spoonfuls at evenly-placed intervals. Bake at 300 degrees Fahrenheit for 55 minutes.

Allow to cool completely before cutting. Store remaining cheesecake (if there's any left!) in the refrigerator.

****

Frozen Blueberry Cream Pie

If you buy a graham cracker crust instead of making your own, this pie takes about 10 minutes to prepare. When I was a kid, we used to go picking blueberries "up north" — which is how I learned to love blueberries and hate wood ticks. (The story is in my book *Where the Green Grass Grows*.)

1 6-ounce package of flavored gelatin (raspberry, black cherry or grape works well)
1 24-ounce carton of low-fat cottage cheese
1 can of blueberry pie filling
1 container of Cool Whip (or other topping)
1 8-9 inch graham cracker crust
several tablespoons of milk

Put the Jell-O, cottage cheese and blueberry pie filling into a blender. Add milk, one tablespoon at a time, and process in the blender. Use only enough milk to liquefy the Jell-O, cottage cheese and pie filling.

Pour into the graham cracker crust. Spread the Cool Whip (or other topping) over the pie filling. Put the pie into the freezer for several hours or overnight. Serve frozen.

Note: For Frozen Cherry Cream Pie use cherry pie filling instead of blueberry.

Extra Note: For a low-fat, sugar-free pie, use sugar-free gelatin and a light whipped topping.

****

Homemade Apple Pie
(No-Roll Pie Crust)

Mix up the no-roll pie crust. (Recipe is below.) Line half of a 10-inch pie plate with the no-roll pie crust and set the other half aside.

Cut up enough apples to make four cups. I never cut the peelings off apples before I use them to make pie or sauce or apple bread. I wash the apples and dry them. Then I cut them up. Apple peelings contain pectin and are a good source of fiber.

Mix one cup of sugar with the apples (or maybe a little more if the apples are very tart) and then mix in 1/4 cup of tapioca. Stir in 1 teaspoon of cinnamon. (If you don't like tapioca, use cornstarch according to the package directions for baking pies.)

Spoon the apple mixture into the pie plate.

Add 1/4 cup of brown sugar to the remaining pie crust mix. Stir thoroughly. Spoon the crumble crust on top of the apples. Bake at 350 degrees Fahrenheit for 60 to 70 minutes (or until crumble crust is golden brown). Allow to cool (at least somewhat!) before cutting.

****

EASY No-Roll Pie Crust
>   3 cups flour
>   1 teaspoon salt
>   2 teaspoons sugar
>   2/3 cup cooking oil (I like to use Canola oil)
>   1/3 cup water or milk

Measure all ingredients into a mixing bowl and stir with a fork. Pat into pie pan with your fingers or use the back of a spoon.

This recipe will make enough for:
• 3 eight-inch one-crust pies (or)
• 2 eight-inch two-crust pies (or)
• 2 ten-inch one-crust pies (or)
• 1 ten-inch two-crust pie with a generous crumble crust.

To make the crumble crust, use half of the mixture for the bottom crust and then add 1/4 cup brown sugar to the remainder and sprinkle on top of your pie filling. For a baked pie shell, bake the crust at 350 degrees Fahrenheit for 15 minutes or until light brown.

****

How to Make Homemade Ice Cream
(Without an Ice Cream Maker!)

Dad's favorite recipe for making ice cream required an ice cream maker. He always made ice cream several times during the summer, for the Fourth of July, birthdays, when we were going to have a picnic in the backyard, or "just because." Much to my regret, I never thought to write down his recipe, but if you would want to make homemade ice cream and don't have the time or the inclination to make it with an ice cream maker, this recipe for ice cream results in a product that is close to the ice cream we ate while I was growing up on our farm.

2 eggs
3/4 cup sugar
2 tablespoons cornstarch
1 cup milk
1 pint whipping cream
pinch of salt
2 teaspoons vanilla

Using an electric mixer, beat the eggs for several minutes until thick and lemon colored. Add 1 cup of milk and blend into the eggs. Mix sugar and cornstarch in a large saucepan. Add egg/milk mixture to the sugar and cornstarch. Cook until thick (about 5 minutes) stirring constantly. Allow the custard mixture to cool to room temperature.

When the custard is cool, put into a freezer-safe bowl. Blend in cream and salt. Freeze for 2 hours or until slushy. Add 2 teaspoons vanilla. Whip for 5 to 10 minutes with an electric mixer. Return to freezer and finish freezing (several hours or overnight).

Variations:
After you have whipped the ice cream, fold in 1 to 2 cups of fresh or frozen fruit, nuts and/or chocolate before returning the ice cream to the freezer to finish freezing. Here are some ideas for additions to your ice cream:
Strawberries
Blackberries
Raspberries
Peaches
Cherries (or Maraschino Cherries)
Chocolate chips
Butterscotch chips
Crushed Heath bars or peppermint candy
Chopped walnuts or pistachio nuts
Coconut
Chocolate chip cookie dough (drop into the ice cream by small spoonfuls and carefully fold in)
Caramel, chocolate or fudge syrup (drop into the ice cream by small amounts and carefully fold in)

****

Homemade Peach Pie
(with No-Roll Pie Crust)

Do you remember buying peaches by the crate during the summer when peaches were in season? You can't buy peaches like that anymore. Every summer when I was growing up, we would get crates of peaches, and my mother and my sister would can them. We also had peach pie. Peaches and cream for dessert. And all the fresh peaches we wanted. If you would rather make a rolled crust, look under "Pie Crust" farther on.

4 cups of cut up peaches
1 cup sugar
2 teaspoons lemon juice
1/2 cup flour (if you do not like to use flour in your pies for thickening, try tapioca or cornstarch and use according to package directions for pies)
1 teaspoon cinnamon (if desired)

Mix up the no-roll pie crust. (Recipe is below.) Line a 10-inch pie plate with half of the no-roll pie crust and set the other half aside.

Measure the peaches into a mixing bowl. Drizzle on the lemon juice and stir thoroughly. Add sugar, flour and cinnamon. Stir thoroughly. Spoon the peach mixture into the pie plate.

Add 1/4 cup of brown sugar to the remaining crust. Mix thoroughly. Spoon the crumble crust on top of the peaches. Bake at 350 degrees Fahrenheit for 60 to 70 minutes (or until crumble crust is golden brown). Allow to cool before cutting. Serve with vanilla ice cream, if desired.

****
EASY No-Roll Pie Crust
3 cups flour
1 teaspoon salt
2 teaspoons sugar
2/3 cup cooking oil (I like to use Canola oil)
1/3 cup water or milk

Measure all ingredients into a mixing bowl and stir with a fork. Pat into pie pan with fingers or use the back of a spoon. Use with your favorite pie recipes. This recipe will make enough for 3 eight-inch one-crust pies (or) 2 eight-inch two-crust pies (or) 2 ten-inch one-crust pies (or) 1 ten-inch two-crust pie with a generous crumble crust.

To make the crumble crust, use half of the mixture for the bottom crust and then add 1/4 cup brown sugar to the remainder and sprinkle on top of your pie filling. For a baked pie shell, bake the crust at 350 degrees for 15 minutes or until light brown.

****

Jam-R-Jelly Parfait Pie

This pie, baked with a no-roll pie crust and a crumble crust top, can be made with any flavor of jam or jelly— grape, strawberry, raspberry, blackberry, chokecherry, wild black cherry, plum. The pie does take a bit of time because first you have to bake the crust and the jam/jelly filling, then you have to add the parfait topping and crumble crust and bake it again. But it's worth the effort! It's especially good if you make your own jam or jelly.

No-roll pie crust (see the previous recipe for peach pie for the no-roll crust)
2 cups of your favorite jam or jelly
1/4 cup water
1 tablespoon lemon juice
1/4 cup cornstarch
(if the jam or jelly is very tart, you might want to add 1/4 cup sugar to the mixture, too)
8 ounces of softened cream cheese
1/2 cup sugar
1 tablespoon lemon juice
1/2 cup sour cream
1 egg

Mix up the no-roll pie crust recipe. Set aside.

Measure the jelly, water, lemon juice and cornstarch (and sometimes sugar) into a mixing bowl and use an electric mixer or a whisk and stir until smooth.

Use half of the no-roll pie crust recipe and press into 9 or 10 inch pie plate. Pour the jam/jelly mixture into the pie crust. Bake at 375 degrees Fahrenheit for 35 to 40 minutes.

Fifteen minutes before the pie comes out of the oven, use an electric mixer to whip the cream cheese, sour cream, sugar, lemon juice and egg until smooth. When the pie comes out of the oven, pour the cream cheese mixture over the jam/jelly filling.

Mix 1/4 cup brown sugar into the remaining no-roll pie crust and sprinkle over the top of the cream cheese mixture.

Bake at 375 degrees for another 25 to 30 minutes.

Allow to cool completely before cutting.

****

Jam-boree Streusel Coffee Cake
(with whole wheat)

When I was growing up on our dairy farm, my mother liked to make coffee cake so Dad would have a treat if he came in the house for morning or afternoon coffee. During the winter, Dad usually came in twice a day for coffee. During the spring and summer when he was busy with fieldwork, sometimes he didn't come in the house for a coffee break at all after breakfast or in the afternoon.

2 cups white flour
1 cup whole wheat flour
1 1/2 cups sugar
3 teaspoons baking powder
1/2 teaspoon salt
1/2 cup Canola oil (or another cooking oil)
1 1/2 cups milk
2 eggs
1 teaspoon vanilla

Streusel
1 cup chopped walnuts
1/2 cup brown sugar
1/2 cup flour
1 teaspoon cinnamon
6 tablespoons butter
**1 to 2 cups jam or jelly (grape, strawberry, raspberry, elderberry, blackberry, plum —
whatever you like)**

Measure coffee cake ingredients into a large mixer bowl. Using an electric mixer, beat on low speed for about a minute to blend ingredients, then beat on medium to high speed for several minutes, scraping the bowl from time to time. Spread half the batter into a greased 9x13 inch pan.

Use a fork to mix the walnuts, brown sugar, flour, cinnamon and butter in a small to medium mixing bowl. Sprinkle half the streusel mixture on top of the batter. Spread the rest of the batter on top of the streusel. Sprinkle the remaining streusel on top of the batter.

Drop the jam or jelly by teaspoonfuls on top of the streusel.

Bake at 350 degrees Fahrenheit for 35 to 40 minutes (until coffee cake is golden brown and feels firm when you tap it with your finger). Allow to cool before cutting.

* *

Marble Bundt Cake

When I was a kid, marble cake was one of my mother's specialties. I was always fascinated with the way that the marble seemed to appear in the cake "like magic." If you need a tremendous amount of cake (such as for a family get-together or a school or church function), this recipe can be doubled and works out fine if you divide the batter between two bundt pans.

    4 cups flour
    2 cups sugar
    3 teaspoons baking powder
    1 teaspoon salt
    3/4 cup milk
    3/4 cup cooking oil
    4 eggs
    2 teaspoons vanilla

Measure all ingredients into a large mixer bowl. Using an electric mixer, stir on low speed for 2 minutes, scraping bowl constantly. Mix on high speed 3 minutes (scrape occasionally).

Spoon 1 cup of batter into a small bowl. Pour half of the remaining batter into a greased bundt pan.

Add 1/4 cup cocoa, 3 tablespoons cooking oil and 1 tablespoon milk to the 1 cup of reserved batter. Mix thoroughly. If desired, add 1/2 cup of coconut to the chocolate mixture.

Pour chocolate batter over the batter in the bundt pan. Pour the remaining white batter over the chocolate batter. Use a butter knife to dip into the batter and "swirl" it, if desired. (Just don't swirl too much or you will end up with a light chocolate bundt cake.) Bake at 350 degrees Fahrenheit for 60 to 70 minutes. Allow to cool thoroughly. Remove the cake from the bundt pan. If desired, frost with a white glaze.

Glaze
    2 cups powdered sugar
    3 tablespoons milk
    1/2 teaspoon vanilla

Combine ingredients and mix thoroughly. If glaze seems too thick to drizzle over the bundt cake, add more milk by teaspoons until the glaze reaches the desired consistency.

If glaze seems too thin, add powdered sugar by tablespoons until it reaches the desired consistency.

****

Mocha Bundt Cake

This recipe makes a very large cake that will fill your bundt pan to the rim (and beyond; because when it's done baking, it will be higher than the rim).

4 cups flour
2 cups sugar
3 teaspoons baking powder
1 teaspoon salt
1/3 cup cocoa (heaping)
1 1/2 cups milk
1/4 cup strong brewed or perked coffee (or use 1 teaspoon instant coffee dissolved in a quarter cup of warm water)
1/2 cup butter
1/2 cup shortening
4 eggs
2 teaspoons vanilla

Measure all ingredients into a large mixing bowl. Using an electric mixer, stir on low speed for several minutes to blend all ingredients. Scrape the bowl while blending. Mix on high speed for a couple of minutes. Scrape the bowl a couple of times while mixing on high speed. Batter will be somewhat stiff when finished.

Grease a 12-cup bundt pan. Spoon the batter into the bundt pan and bake at 350 degrees Fahrenheit for 65 to 70 minutes or until a toothpick inserted into the cake comes out clean.

Allow to cool before removing cake from the pan.

Frost with the glaze from the previous recipe for Marble Bundt Cake, if desired. To make a chocolate glaze, add 1 to 2 tablespoons of cocoa to the recipe. Drizzle on cake. Sprinkle with coconut before the glaze sets, if you want.

****

Old-Fashioned Oatmeal Spice Cake

One of my mother's favorite cakes was oatmeal spice cake. When I was a kid, I did not especially think it was anything special, but I sure do like it now…

1 cup brown sugar
1 cup white sugar
2 eggs
1/2 cup of shortening
1 cup dry oatmeal (quick-cooking or old-fashioned)
1 1/4 cups boiling water
2 cups flour
1 teaspoon baking soda
1/2 teaspoon salt
1/2 teaspoon cinnamon
1/2 teaspoon all-spice
1 teaspoon vanilla

Topping
(to be added <u>before</u> the cake is baked)
3/4 cup brown sugar
1 cup coconut
1 cup chopped walnuts
1 egg
3 tablespoons melted butter
3 tablespoons milk

Measure dry oatmeal into a small bowl and pour boiling water over the oatmeal. Let sit for 10 minutes.

Using an electric mixer, cream brown sugar, white sugar, shortening and eggs. Add the oatmeal. Add the remaining dry ingredients and the vanilla. Mix on low speed for a minute to blend ingredients. Mix on high speed for a couple of minutes, scraping bowl occasionally. Spoon into a 9x13 inch greased pan.

To make the topping, beat the egg with a fork, then add the remaining ingredients and stir thoroughly. Drop the topping onto the cake batter by forkfuls. Use the fork to spread out the topping.

Bake at 350 degrees Fahrenheit for 35 to 40 minutes or until a toothpick comes out clean.

****

Pancake Mix Dessert

This was one of my mother's favorite recipes when she needed a dessert in a hurry.

3/4 stick of butter
1 cup of dry pancake mix
1 can of pie filling (any flavor)

Melt 3/4 of a stick of butter in a 9 x 9 or 8 x 8 inch square pan. Sprinkle 1 cup of dry pancake mix over the melted butter. Spread 1 can of pie filling (any flavor) over the pancake mix. Blueberry or cherry pie filling works especially well.

Bake in a 350 degree Fahrenheit oven for 30 minutes.

✳✳✳✳✳✳✳✳✳✳✳✳✳✳✳✳✳✳✳✳

"Easy as Pie" Dessert

Here is another easy dessert recipe. For an added treat, sprinkle with coconut before freezing.

Graham crackers
2 packages of instant pudding (3 ounce size; or 1 6-ounce size)— any flavor
3 cups milk
1 large container (or 2 smaller containers) of Cool Whip or another whipped topping

Line the bottom of a 9x13 pan with graham cracker squares. Mix the pudding and the milk until it starts to set. Blend in 1/2 of the big container or 1 of the small containers of whipped topping. Spread pudding and whipped topping mixture over the graham crackers. Top with another layer of graham crackers. Cover with another layer of whipped topping. Sprinkle with coconut if desired. Freeze for 4 to 6 hours or overnight. Remove from the freezer 1 hour before serving.

To make a smaller dessert, cut the recipe in half and use an 8x8 or 9x9 pan.

Instead of whipped topping, you can make a richer dessert by using whipped cream, if you want.
1 pint of whipping cream; 1/2 cup sugar. Pour the cream into a metal bowl and, using an electric, mixer, whip on high speed until cream begins to thicken. Gradually add 1/2 cup sugar while whipping. Continue whipping until thick.

✳✳✳✳✳✳✳✳✳✳✳✳✳✳✳✳✳✳✳✳

Pie Crust
(Make Ahead)

If you would rather roll out your own pie crust instead of using the "no-roll" pie crust recipe included with my other pie recipes, this mix-ahead recipe makes enough crust for three or four two-crust pies depending on the size of the pie plate.

6 cups flour
2 1/2 cups shortening
2 teaspoons salt

Measure the ingredients into a large mixing bowl and work together with a fork.

Place dry mixture in an air-tight container and refrigerate.

For a two-crust pie:
2 cups of mix
1/3 cup milk

****

Pie Crust for One-Crust Pie (10-inch)

1 1/3 cup flour
1/2 teaspoon salt
1/2 cup shortening
4 tablespoons cold water

Measure flour, salt, and shortening into a mixing bowl. Work together with a fork. Add cold water by the tablespoon and mix together until the dough reaches the right consistency.

Double the recipe for a two-crust pie.

****

Rhubarb Coffee Cake

When I was a kid, we used to go to another farm owned by some friends to cut rhubarb. When my mom and dad retired from farming and built a house at the back of the farm, Dad planted several Canadian Red rhubarb plants. Today, nearly 35 years later, the Canadian Red rhubarb is still growing. My husband and I moved it out of the horse pasture and planted it up by the barn, and it is thriving. Canadian red works well in this cake and makes it more colorful.

1 1/2 cups brown sugar
1/2 cup shortening
1 egg
1 cup of buttermilk (or 1 cup sweet milk to which you have added 1 tablespoon of vinegar or lemon juice)
1 teaspoon baking soda
1/4 teaspoon salt
2 cups flour
1 1/2 cups raw rhubarb cut up into fine pieces

Topping
1/2 cup brown sugar
1/2 teaspoon cinnamon
1/2 cup chopped walnuts
2 tablespoons flour

Measure the sugar and shortening into a mixing bowl. Cream together. Beat in the egg. Add the buttermilk/sour milk, baking soda, salt and flour. Beat until smooth. Stir in the rhubarb.

Spoon the batter into a greased 9 x 13 pan.

Measure the brown sugar, cinnamon, chopped nuts and flour into a small mixing bowl. Stir until thoroughly combined. Sprinkle on top of cake batter.

Bake at 350 degrees Fahrenheit for 45 minutes.

* * * * * * * * * * * * * * * * * * *

Rhubarb Cream Pie

This is a somewhat different kind of rhubarb pie with strawberry Jell-O, marshmallows and whipped cream.

Crust:
2 cups crushed graham crackers
1/4 cup sugar
1/2 cup butter (melted)

Pie filling:
4 cups rhubarb cut into small pieces
2 cups sugar
1 package of strawberry gelatin
1 cup miniature marshmallows
1 cup of whipping cream (whipped with a 1/4 cup sugar)

Mix the graham cracker crumbs, sugar and melted butter in a small mixing bowl. Press into a 10-inch pie plate with your fingers or the back of a spoon.

Cook the rhubarb and sugar in a saucepan over medium heat until the rhubarb has turned to mush. Stir constantly to make sure that the mixture does not stick to the pan. Add the strawberry gelatin and stir until it is completely dissolved. Allow to cool for 10 minutes.

Add the miniature marshmallows to the rhubarb mixture and stir until melted. Let cool completely.

Use an electric mixer to whip the cream in a mixing bowl. Gradually stir in 1/4 cup sugar and continue whipping until it reaches the desired consistency. Fold the whipped cream into the rhubarb mixture.

Spoon the rhubarb and whipped cream into the crust. Refrigerate until set.

****

Rhubarb Custard Pie

My dad liked any kind of custard pie or cream pie, and as long as it was sweet enough, this Rhubarb Custard Pie was good, too, as far as he was concerned.

Pie filling:
2 eggs
2 tablespoons milk
2 cups sugar
1/4 cup flour
1/2 teaspoon nutmeg
3 cups rhubarb (cut into small pieces)

Topping:
1/2 cup brown sugar
2/3 cup flour
1/4 cup butter

Pie crust:
1 1/3 cups flour
1/2 teaspoon salt
1/2 cup shortening
4 tablespoons cold water

Make the pie crust (8 to 10 inch pie plate). Measure flour, salt, and shortening into a mixing bowl. Work together with a fork. Add cold water by the tablespoon and mix together until the dough reaches the right consistency. Roll out the dough and put in the pie plate. Use a fork to crimp the edges of the pie crust against the pan.

Pie filling: Beat eggs and milk together in a mixing bowl. Stir in the sugar, flour and nutmeg (mixture will be very thick). Stir in the rhubarb. Spoon the rhubarb mixture into the pie crust.

Topping: Mix the brown sugar, flour and butter in a small bowl. As you would for pie crust, work together with a fork. Sprinkle over the pie filling.

Bake at 375 degrees Fahrenheit for 50 to 60 minutes.

****

Rhubarb Crisp (or Apple Crisp)

This recipe can also be used to make apple crisp, or if you can find some really good ones (hard to do in the store nowadays), peaches would work well, too.

Crust:
    4 cups flour
    1 cup white sugar
    1 cup brown sugar
    1/2 cup butter
    1 cup shortening
    1/2 teaspoon salt

Filling:
    6 cups of rhubarb cut into small pieces
    2 cups sugar
    1/2 cup of flour
    1/2 teaspoon cinnamon (if desired)

Using a fork, mix the flour, white sugar, brown sugar, butter, shortening and salt until crumbly.

Put half of the mixture into the bottom of a lightly greased 9x13 pan. Pat down firmly with the back of a spoon or use your fingers. Bake the crust in a 350 degree Fahrenheit oven for 10 minutes.

While the crust is baking, mix the rhubarb with 2 cups of sugar and 1/2 cup flour.

Put the rhubarb mixture on top of the crust. Sprinkle the rest of the crust mixture on top of the rhubarb.

Bake in a 350 degree Fahrenheit oven for 45 to 50 minutes.

Apple Crisp or Peach Crisp:
Make the crust in exactly the same way, but instead of rhubarb use 6 cups of apples or peaches cut up into small pieces, 1 cup of sugar (if the apples or peaches are tart, use 2 cups), 1/2 cup flour and 1 teaspoon cinnamon. Bake the bottom crust for 10 minutes. Add the apple mixture and the topping. Bake at 350 degrees Fahrenheit for 45 to 50 minutes.

****

Royal Rhubarb Pie
(with Easy No-Roll Pie Crust)

Filling:
    2 tablespoons water
    4 cups rhubarb (cut up)
    2 cups sugar
    1/4 cup cornstarch
    a pinch of salt
    1/2 cup milk (cream, or Half & Half)

Note: If you're using the 'old-fashioned' rhubarb with the greenish stalks, add several drops of red food coloring. If you are using the Canadian Red rhubarb, there's no need for food coloring.

Make pie crust (see below) and bake the bottom shell at 350 degrees Fahrenheit for 15 minutes.

While the pie shell is baking, put rhubarb, 1 3/4 cups sugar and 2 tablespoons of water into a saucepan and cook over medium heat for 10 minutes, stirring constantly. Remove from burner. Mix 1/4 cup sugar with 1/4 cup cornstarch and stir into the hot rhubarb mixture. Add milk (cream or Half & Half). Cook until thick.

Pour filling into the baked pie shell. Add crumble crust. Bake at 350 degrees Fahrenheit for 20 minutes until crust is lightly browned. Allow to cool thoroughly before cutting. Serve with whipped cream or vanilla ice cream if desired.

* * * * * * * * * * * * * * * * *

Pie Crust:
    3 cups flour
    1 teaspoon salt
    2 teaspoons sugar
    2/3 cup cooking oil (I like to use Canola oil)
    1/3 cup water or milk

Measure all ingredients into a mixing bowl and work together with a fork. Put half of the mixture into a 10-inch pie plate and pat down with the back of a spoon (or use your fingers) to form the pie crust. Bake at 350 degrees Fahrenheit for 15 minutes.

Mix 1/4 cup of brown sugar with the remaining pie crust and sprinkle on top of pie to form a "crumble crust." (Makes a generous crumble crust). Bake in a 350 degree oven for 20 minutes or until the crumble crust is slightly browned.

* * * * * * * * * * * * * * * * * * * *

Small Rhubarb Crisp

This rhubarb crisp is baked in a casserole dish. The recipes works especially well if you are only serving a few people.

1/2 cup of dry oatmeal
1 cup brown sugar
1/2 cup flour
1 stick of softened butter
4 cups of rhubarb cut into small pieces
1 1/2 cups sugar

Measure oatmeal, brown sugar, flour and butter into a mixing bowl and use a fork to cut in the butter until it resembles coarse meal.

Press half of the crust mixture into an 8 x 8 inch casserole dish.

Mix the rhubarb and sugar until thoroughly combined. Spoon the rhubarb over the crust.

Sprinkle remaining crust on top of the rhubarb.

Bake at 350 degrees Fahrenheit for 40 to 45 minutes.

****

Strawberries and Cream Pie

When I was a little girl, we used to go to a strawberry farm to pick strawberries in June. Dad also planted strawberries in the garden one year. If the berries were particularly large, he would call them "punkins."

Note: you can also use frozen strawberries with this recipe, although you may have to add a teaspoon or two more of cornstarch to thicken the filling.

Filling:
   2 tablespoons water
   4 cups strawberries (sliced)
   1 1/2 cups sugar
   1/4 cup cornstarch (heaping)
   a pinch of salt
   1/2 cup sour cream

Make pie crust (see below) and bake the bottom shell at 350 degrees Fahrenheit for 15 minutes.

While the pie shell is baking, put strawberries, 1 cup sugar and 2 tablespoons of water into a saucepan and cook over medium heat for 10 minutes, stirring constantly. Remove from burner.

Mix 1/2 cup sugar with 1/4 cup cornstarch (heaping) and stir into the hot strawberry mixture. Add sour cream. Cook until thick.

Pour filling into the baked pie shell. Add crumble crust. Bake at 350 degrees for 20 minutes until crust is lightly browned. Allow to cool thoroughly before cutting. Serve with whipped cream or vanilla ice cream, if you like.

* * * * * * * * * * * * * * * * *

Pie Crust:
   3 cups flour
   1 teaspoon salt
   2 teaspoons sugar
   2/3 cup cooking oil (I like to use Canola oil)
   1/3 cup water or milk

Measure all ingredients into a mixing bowl and work together with a fork. Put half of the mixture into a 10-inch pie plate and pat down with the back of a spoon (or use your fingers) to form the pie crust. Bake at 350 degrees Fahrenheit for 15 minutes.

* * * * * * * * * * * * * * * * * * * *

Strawberry Rhubarb Coffee Cake

Note: Be sure to use at least 4 cups of cut up rhubarb, otherwise the cake tends to be a little dry. Also, if you want, substitute 2/3 cup of Canola oil (or another vegetable oil) for the butter in the bottom layer.

Bottom Layer:
  1/2 cup butter or margarine (or 2/3 cup of Canola oil or another vegetable oil)
  1 cup sugar
  2 cups flour
  1/2 teaspoon salt
  1 teaspoon baking powder
  1/4 cup milk
  2 eggs
  1 teaspoon vanilla

Cream shortening and sugar. Beat in eggs and stir in milk. Add dry ingredients. Mix until smooth. (Batter will be stiff.) Spread in the bottom of greased 9x13 pan.

Middle Layer:
  4 to 5 cups of rhubarb (cut up)
  2 eggs
  1/4 cup milk
  2 cups sugar
  1 cup flour
  1 three-ounce package strawberry gelatin (raspberry or black cherry works too)

Measure rhubarb into a mixing bowl. Stir in eggs, milk, sugar and flour. Spread over bottom layer. Sprinkle the dry strawberry Jell-O over the rhubarb mixture.

Top Layer:
  1 cup flour
  3/4 cup brown sugar
  1/2 cup butter or margarine

Put all ingredients into a mixing bowl. Use a fork to cut the butter into the flour and brown sugar. Continue mixing until crumbly. Sprinkle over the rhubarb layer.

Bake at 350 degrees Fahrenheit for 70 minutes or until a knife inserted in the center comes out clean.

＊＊＊＊＊＊＊＊＊＊＊＊＊＊＊＊＊＊＊＊

Strawberry Shortcake

Over the years, I have noticed there are two philosophies for Strawberry Shortcake. There are the people who make Strawberry Shortcake with biscuits. And those who make it with angel food cake. My mother belonged to the biscuit philosophy. My husband comes from an angel-food-cake-for-strawberry-shortcake background.

3 cups flour
1/2 cup shortening
3 teaspoons baking powder
1/2 teaspoon salt
1 to 2 tablespoons of sugar (use 2 if you want your biscuits sweeter)
1 cup milk

Measure the flour, shortening baking powder, sugar and salt into a mixing bowl. Cut the shortening into the flour with a fork until it resembles coarse meal. Gradually stir in the milk to form the dough. If the dough seems too dry, add milk by tablespoons. If the dough seems too soft, add flour by the quarter cup.

Knead the dough on a floured surface for a minute or so. Then roll out to a half-inch thick and make biscuits with a biscuit cutter or donut cutter or round cookie cutter.

Bake on an ungreased cookie sheet at 350 degrees Fahrenheit for 20 or 25 minutes or until golden brown.

Makes about 12 to 18 biscuits, depending on the size of the cutter you use.

Strawberries:
4 cups of fresh strawberries (or thawed frozen strawberries)
1 cup of sugar (or to taste)

Crush the strawberries. Stir in the sugar until dissolved. Serve over baking powder biscuits and topped with whipped cream. Yum!

****

Twinkie Filling

This recipe can be used as frosting and/or filling for a cake, or you can also use it as filling for a jelly roll.

1/4 cup butter
1/2 cup shortening
1 cup white sugar
3/4 cup evaporated milk
1 teaspoon vanilla

Measure all ingredients into a mixing bowl and whip together until fluffy.

Use as a filling for a sponge cake or use to frost a 9 x 13 cake or a layer cake.

****

Walnut (or Pecan) Pie

This is a sure-fire recipe for walnut or pecan pie. I like to make the pie with walnuts, probably because I most often have walnuts on hand. When I was a kid, Dad loved walnuts. For a snack after the evening milking sometimes, he would help himself to a handful of walnuts from the bag my mother always kept in the cupboard for baking.

> **1 cup white corn syrup**
> **1 cup brown sugar**
> **1/3 teaspoon salt**
> **1/3 cup melted butter**
> **1 teaspoon vanilla**
> **3 whole eggs**
> **1 heaping cup of walnut or pecan halves**

Measure the syrup, sugar, salt, butter, and vanilla into a mixing bowl and stir until thoroughly combined. Put the eggs in a small mixing bowl and beat with a fork. Stir the eggs into the syrup mixture. Pour into a 9-inch unbaked pie crust.

Sprinkle the nuts over the filling. Use more than a cup if takes that many to cover the top of the filling. Bake at 350 degrees Fahrenheit for 45 minutes or until a knife inserted into the center of the pie comes out clean.

Allow to cool before cutting.

****

White Frosting

My sister used to make a frosting like this for my birthday cakes when I was a kid. Do you remember when birthday cakes were a really BIG DEAL? I do. It was fun to know that someone was baking a cake just for me and that it would be slathered with fluffy, sweet white frosting.

1/2 cup milk
1/4 cup flour
1/4 cup plus 1 tablespoon shortening
1/2 cup sugar
1/8 teaspoon salt
1 to 2 teaspoons of vanilla
1 to 2 cups of powdered sugar

Measure flour into a small saucepan. Add milk, by tablespoons, and stir until the mixture is smooth. Cook over medium heat, stirring constantly, until the mixture thickens.

Set paste aside until it is cold.

Put the cold paste into a mixing bowl. Add shortening, sugar and vanilla, and use an electric mixer to beat until smooth. Gradually beat in 1 to 2 cups of powdered sugar until the frosting reaches the desired consistency.

Chocolate Frosting:

Add 1/4 cup to a 1/2 cup of cocoa and beat until smooth. If the frosting seems like it is becoming too stiff, add milk by the tablespoon until the frosting reaches the desired consistency.

* * * * * * * * * * * * * * * * * * * *

Candy

Candied Orange Peel

As far as my mother was concerned, Candied Orange Peel was a true delicacy. My mother was born in 1916, and oranges were few and far between when she was a girl. If you could find oranges to buy, and you could afford them, you wanted to make sure that you used every bit. I have to confess, though, that I like Candied Orange Peel too! It's a little labor intensive, but it's worth it, I think.

When you are peeling your oranges to eat them, save the peeling and set aside in a bowl. If you are eating oranges in the winter, the orange peel will be fine in the bowl just sitting on the cupboard for a few days.

After you have accumulated several cups of orange peel, trim off the ragged edges and cut into small pieces about a half inch by a half inch.

Measure five or six cups of water into a large kettle and add the orange peel. Simmer for a half hour. Drain off the water. Add six more cups of water to the kettle and simmer again for a half hour. Dump orange peel into a colander and allow to drain thoroughly.

Measure 2 cups of sugar and 1 cup of water into another kettle and heat to boiling. Add the orange peel. Simmer over low heat for about 1 hour, stirring frequently.

Dump the orange peel into the colander again and allow the syrup to drain off thoroughly. When the orange peel is drained, roll the orange peel in white sugar and spread on an ungreased cookie sheet or on waxed paper and allow to dry.

The orange peel is not going to dry completely but will remain rather sticky.

This is good to eat (like candy) but you can also use it to decorate a cake after you have frosted it with white frosting. To use on a cake, chop into very small pieces and sprinkle over the frosting.

****

Caramel Popcorn

Caramel Popcorn was Mom's favorite. I like it, too! This is a rich, buttery recipe that I save for special occasions, like Christmas.

8 cups of popped corn

3/4 cup white sugar
3/4 cup packed brown sugar
1/2 cup light corn syrup
1/2 cup water
1 teaspoon vinegar
3/4 cup of butter or 2 tablespoons of butter and 1/3 to 1/2 cup butterscotch chips

Measure the white sugar, brown sugar, corn syrup, water and vinegar into a fairly large saucepan. Heat to boiling over medium heat, stirring quite often.

Boil and stir constantly until the mixture reaches 235 to 240 degrees Fahrenheit on a candy thermometer or until a small amount dropped into ice water forms a small ball.

Turn heat down to low and stir in the butter. If you don't want to use so much butter, use 2 tablespoons of butter and 1/3 cup to a 1/2 cup of butterscotch chips. Stir the butter (or the butter and butterscotch chips) into the hot mixture and stir until melted.

Measure the popcorn into a large bowl. Pour the syrup over the popcorn, stirring constantly so that the popcorn becomes coated with the syrup.

Grease a cookie sheet and dump the popcorn out onto the cookie sheet and spread it out. Allow to cool. Break it up into pieces and store in plastic bags or containers.

If you would rather make popcorn balls, instead of spreading the popcorn mixture out on a cookie sheet, rub the palms of your hand with butter and shape into balls and set on wax paper.

****

Cherry Chocolate Marshmallow Pizza

This is certain to satisfy even the biggest sweet tooth. And I ought to know, because I've got just about the biggest sweet tooth you'll find anywhere — like many Norwegians.

1 twelve-ounce package of milk chocolate chips
1 pound of white almond bark
2 cups of colored miniature marshmallows
1 cup of crispy rice cereal (Rice Krispies or a generic brand)
1 1/2 cups of dry roasted peanuts
1 small container of red candied cherries
1 small container of green candied cherries
1 cup shredded coconut
1 teaspoon cooking oil

Dump the chocolate chips into a microwave safe bowl. Cut the pound of almond bark into two blocks of 2/3 and 1/3. Break up the 2/3 pound of almond bark and add to the bowl with the chocolate chips. Microwave for several minutes to melt the chips and the almond bark.

When the chips and almond bark are melted, mix the contents of the bowl until thoroughly combined. Stir in the marshmallows, cereal and peanuts and mix until thoroughly combined.

Spoon the chocolate mixture onto a lightly greased pizza pan. Cut the red and green cherries into small chunks. Sprinkle (as best you can because candied cherries are sticky) the cherry bits onto the chocolate.

Sprinkle the coconut over the cherry bits and chocolate.

Place the remaining almond bark in a microwave safe bowl along with 1 teaspoon of cooking oil. Melt the almond bark. When it is melted, drizzle the almond bark over the chocolate mixture in the pizza pan. When the "pizza" is cool, break into pieces to serve. Or cut it into pieces with a sharp knife or a pizza cutter.

Store at room temperature in a loosely covered container.

****

Divinity
(The Easier Way!)

When I was a kid, someone always made divinity and brought it for the lunch served after the Sunday school Christmas program. I loved the stuff. When I grew older, I wanted to make divinity, too. The old-fashioned way is to cook the syrup, beat the egg whites until stiff, and then pour the hot syrup over the egg whites in a thin stream while beating with an electric mixer on high speed. I tried it when I was old enough to operate the mixer. And I ended up burning out my mother's electric mixer.

This version is an easier way to make divinity. It doesn't taste exactly like the real thing, but it looks like divinity, and at least you won't be buying a new electric mixer when you're finished! For a festive touch, add a few drops of red or green food coloring if desired.

1 package of white frosting mix (7.5 ounces)
2 tablespoons white corn syrup
1 teaspoon vanilla
1 1/2 cups powdered sugar
1/2 cup chopped walnuts

Prepare the frosting according to the package directions.

When the frosting is sufficiently fluffy, beat in the 2 tablespoons of corn syrup on high speed. Add the vanilla and beat. If desired, add the red or green food coloring and beat in.

Stir in the powdered sugar by 1/2 cup-fulls. You can begin with the electric mixer to beat in the powdered sugar, but by the last 1/2 cup, you may have to work it in with your fingers or use dough hook. Stir in (or work in) the walnuts.

Drop by small spoonfuls onto wax paper. Let dry for 12 to 24 hours. When the candy is dry to the touch, turn it over and let it dry for another 12 to 24 hours.

Store in a loosely covered container with wax paper between the layers.

****

Heath Bars

This recipe uses saltine crackers, and the resulting "Heath" bars are very good. This is an easy recipe and takes about 20 minutes from start to finish. The longest (and hardest) part of it all is waiting for the bars to cool off enough so you can eat them!

1 to 2 packages of saltine crackers (not boxes of crackers, but the individual packages of crackers that come in the boxes)
1 cup brown sugar
1 cup of butter
1 twelve-ounce package of milk chocolate chips or semi-sweet chocolate chips (you can also use butterscotch chips, if you prefer, or mix the butterscotch and chocolate chips)
1 cup of finely chopped walnuts, pecans or almonds

Line a 10x15-inch jelly roll pan with aluminum foil. Grease the aluminum foil lightly with shortening. Lay the crackers side by side until the bottom of the pan is covered.

Measure the brown sugar and butter into a medium-sized saucepan and boil over medium-high heat for 3 minutes, stirring constantly.

Pour the brown sugar and butter mixture over the crackers. Bake at 350 degrees Fahrenheit for 8 to 10 minutes.

Sprinkle the chocolate chips on top of the cracker mixture immediately after removing the pan from the oven. Use the back of a spoon or a knife to spread the chocolate chips when melted.

Sprinkle the chopped nuts over the chocolate before the chocolate cools and sets.

I have also melted white almond bark and have drizzled that over the chocolate.

Allow to cool completely before cutting or breaking into pieces.

****

Loretta's Chocolate Bonbons

(as mentioned in the story "Good Things Come in Small Packages" in my book
Christmas in Dairyland — True Stories from a Wisconsin Farm)

1 1/2 cups shredded coconut
1 stick butter
2 pounds powdered sugar
1 can sweetened condensed milk
2 cups chopped nuts
1 1/2 teaspoons vanilla
1 large package chocolate chips
2/3 bar paraffin
(Instead of chocolate chips and paraffin, the coconut balls can be dipped in melted chocolate almond bark.)

Mix coconut, butter, powdered sugar, condensed milk, nuts and vanilla. Roll into small balls. Chill in refrigerator for several hours or in the freezer for one hour.

Melt chocolate chips and paraffin in a double boiler (or in a clean coffee can set on canning jar rings in a pan of water). Using a toothpick, dip the chilled coconut balls into the chocolate mixture. Place on wax paper until set.

****

Marshmallow Fudge

To me, Christmas does not seem like Christmas without fudge. In the "good old days," my big sister would make fudge the by cooking the mixture, placing the pan in ice water and beating the fudge until it was ready to be put in a 9 x 13 pan. This recipe for fudge is much easier — and just as tasty.

3 cups sugar
3/4 cup butter
1 cup evaporated milk
1 teaspoon vanilla
1 twelve-ounce bag of semi-sweet chocolate chips
1/2 bag of marshmallows (or 2 cups) (regular or miniature)
1 cup chopped walnuts (optional)

Measure the sugar, butter and milk into a medium-sized saucepan. Bring to a full, rolling boil over medium-high heat, stirring constantly. Boil for 5 minutes. Keep stirring so the mixture does not scorch on the bottom of the pan. You may want to turn the heat down if the mixture begins to stick too much.

Remove the pan from the heat and stir in the chocolate chips. Continuing stirring until the chocolate chips are melted. Add the marshmallows, vanilla and chopped nuts (if desired), and stir until the marshmallows are melted. Pour into a greased 9x13 pan. Cool to room temperature and then chill in the refrigerator. Cut into pieces.

Note: if you are using regular marshmallows instead of miniature, you might want to cut the marshmallows up into small pieces before adding to the fudge so they will melt faster.

****

Peanut Butter Treats

These tasty treats are somewhat time-consuming, but they're quite delicious. I made them one time when my mother was serving Ladies Aid at our house. The ladies loved them, one in particular who described them as "sumptuous chocolate tarts."

2 eight-ounce chocolate candy bars (Hershey bars work well)
1 cup peanut butter (smooth or chunky)
1 dozen cupcake papers
3/4 cup peanut butter (smooth or chunky)

Put cupcake papers into muffin tin cups.

Break the chocolate bars into pieces and place in a saucepan. Add 1 cup of peanut butter. Warm over medium heat until melted, stirring constantly. Or put in a microwave safe bowl and put in the microwave until the chocolate and peanut butter are melted.

Put one three-quarters of a tablespoon of the chocolate and peanut butter mixture into each of the muffin papers.

Set the pan aside.

Measure 3/4 cup of peanut butter into another saucepan or a microwave-safe bowl. Heat the peanut butter until it is melted.

Pour 3/4 quarters of tablespoon of melted peanut butter over the chocolate mixture in the cupcake papers.

Chill in the refrigerator for 15 minutes.

While the chocolate and peanut butter mixture is chilling, warm up the remainder of the chocolate and peanut butter mixture until melted again.

Put 3/4 of a tablespoon of chocolate and peanut butter mixture over the other ingredients in the cupcake papers.

Chill until set.

****

Peanut Butter Fudge

I don't know if it is proper to call this candy "fudge" since it does not have any cocoa or chocolate, but it definitely satisfies a sweet tooth!

2 cups sugar
2/3 cup milk
1 cup marshmallow cream
1 cup smooth peanut butter
1 teaspoon vanilla

Measure the sugar and milk into a saucepan and cook over medium heat, stirring constantly, until it reaches the soft ball stage (a drop of the mixture in cold water holds its shape) (or used a candy thermometer). Remove from heat. Set aside.

Measure marshmallow cream, peanut butter and vanilla into a mixing bowl. Pour half of the cooked mixture over the marshmallow, peanut butter and vanilla and stir until thoroughly combined. Add the remainder of the cooked mixture and stir until thoroughly combined.

Spoon into a greased 9 x 13 pan . Cool in the refrigerator. Cut into squares. Store in the refrigerator.

****

Saltwater Taffy

When I was a kid, my best friend would come over on a Sunday afternoon, and sometimes we would make taffy. My mother used to tell me about taffy pulls they would have at school, too, when she was a girl and how much fun it was to make taffy. Mom went to school in a little one-room country school about a mile from our farm.

1 cup sugar
3/4 cup light corn syrup
2/3 cup water
1 tablespoon cornstarch
2 tablespoons butter
3/4 teaspoon salt
2 teaspoons vanilla (or another flavoring, such as peppermint or anise; I like vanilla.)

In a large saucepan, combine all ingredients except the vanilla. Stirring constantly, cook over medium heat until the mixture reaches 256 degrees Fahrenheit on a candy thermometer (or until a small amount dropped into a cup of cold water forms a hard ball).

Stir in vanilla. Pour into a buttered 8x8 square pan. Let cool.

Note: if you would like to make colored taffy, stir in a few drops of food coloring just before you add the vanilla or other flavoring.

When the mixture is cool enough to handle, rub a small amount of soft butter between your palms, take a handful of taffy and pull until it becomes stiff and lighter in color. Pull or roll into ropes and cut into pieces with a scissors.

To store the candy, let it sit for an hour or so and then wrap the individual pieces in plastic wrap or waxed paper.

****

Sweet Adelines

You can put this candy into an 8x8-inch pan and frost with chocolate frosting or melted chocolate chips —or you can roll it into balls and dip it into melted chocolate almond bark.

1 package of white frosting mix (7.5 ounce box)
2 tablespoons of milk or water
1/2 cup peanut butter (crunchy or smooth)
3/4 cup marshmallows
3 cups crispy rice cereal
1/2 cup chopped dry roasted peanuts

Dump the dry frosting mix into a microwave-safe bowl. Add the milk, peanut butter and marshmallows. Use a spoon to mix the frosting, milk, peanut butter and marshmallows.

Microwave for one minute or until the peanut butter and marshmallows are melted.

Stir in the cereal and the peanuts.

Spoon into a lightly greased 8x8 inch pan.

If desired, melt a six-ounce package of chocolate chips and spread over the candy. Allow the melted chocolate chips to set before cutting.

To make the candy into balls, roll by teaspoonfuls into small balls and place on wax paper. Dip balls into melted chocolate almond bark. Place back on wax paper until set. Store in a loosely covered container with wax paper between the layers.

****

Casseroles
and
Main Dishes

Baked Beans

If you've ever made your own baked beans, you know there is no comparison to the baked beans you buy in cans. For one thing, homemade baked beans make the kitchen smell good for a long, long time, seeing as they take hours to bake. This is how my mother made baked beans when I was a kid.

2 pounds Great Northern beans
1/2 cup chopped onion
several slices of lean bacon (cut into small pieces)
1 1/2 to 2 teaspoons salt
1/2 cup molasses
2 teaspoons dry mustard
1/2 cup catsup
1 cup brown sugar

Put the beans in a Dutch oven or kettle. Cover with water. Soak overnight. Drain the beans and cover with fresh water. Bring to a boil. Cook for 10 minutes. Let the beans cool off for 30 minutes. Drain the water off the beans.

Stir together the salt, molasses, dry mustard, catsup and brown sugar.

Put the beans in a casserole dish. Stir in the bacon pieces. Add enough fresh water just to cover the beans. Stir in the molasses, catsup and brown sugar mixture.

Bake at 300 degrees for 6 to 8 hours or until the beans are tender. If the beans start to dry out, stir in more water as needed.

****

Barbecued Beef

This is one way to use leftover roast beef.

1 tablespoon vinegar
1 1/2 cups water
1 tablespoon brown sugar
1 tablespoon molasses
1/2 teaspoon ground mustard
1/4 teaspoon salt (or to taste)
1 medium onion, chopped
1/2 cup catsup
3 tablespoons Worcestershire sauce (optional)
4 to 6 cups of cooked, shredded beef

Combine vinegar, water, brown sugar, mustard, and onion in a saucepan. Simmer for 20 minutes. Add catsup (and Worcestershire sauce). Stir until thoroughly combined.

Pour sauce over beef and mix thoroughly. Refrigerate for at least several hours.

Slowly simmer the beef mixture for 30 to 45 minutes before serving.

Serve on hamburger buns. A slotted spoon works well to serve the meat so that the mixture isn't too mushy and wet for the buns.

****

Barbecued Chicken

When I was a very little girl, we had chickens on our farm. We had a chicken coop, but because of the way it was situated next to the barnyard, Dad said there was no room to build an enclosure for them to keep them near the chicken coop. After a while my mother grew tired of chicken manure deposited around the yard being dragged into the house on shoes. So that was the end of the chickens. We bought eggs after that from a neighbor who kept chickens after that.

1/2 cup butter
1 1/2 cups chopped onion
1 clove of garlic, chopped (or you can use garlic powder, if you prefer)
2 cups of stewed tomatoes (mashed or put through a blender)
1 cup tomato paste
2 tablespoons brown sugar
2 tablespoons Worcestershire sauce (if desired)
1 teaspoon dry mustard
1 teaspoon salt
2 cut up fryer chickens (or 4 chicken breasts)

Melt butter and sauté the onion and garlic until tender. Stir in the stewed tomatoes and tomato paste, brown sugar, Worcestershire sauce, mustard and salt. Simmer for about 15 minutes.

Cook the chicken on a charcoal or gas grill, turning every 10 minutes and basting with barbecue sauce the last 1/2 of the cooking time.

Chicken may also be baked in a casserole dish in the oven for 1 and 1/2 hours or until tender at 350 degrees Fahrenheit. Pour the barbecue sauce over the chicken. Baste several times while the chicken is in the oven.

****

Beef Burgundy
(Easy Recipe!)

This is a good recipe for stew meat or for steak that is a little on the tough side and needs help. If you do not want the extra salt from the bouillon and soy sauce, use water and add a small amount of salt.

2 to 3 tablespoons shortening
2 pounds of sirloin steak or 2 pounds of well-trimmed stew meat
1 small to medium onion, chopped
1 cup of beef bouillon
1/2 cup cranberry juice (or grape juice or Burgundy wine, if desired)
2 teaspoons soy sauce
1 clove of chopped garlic (or garlic powder to taste)
2 tablespoons of cornstarch
1/4 cup water
4 cups cooked rice

Cut sirloin into one-inch pieces (or trim stew meat). In a heavy skillet, brown meat and the chopped onion in melted shortening. Stir in beef bouillon, cranberry juice (or wine), soy sauce and garlic. Cover and simmer until meat is tender.

Stir the cornstarch into the 1/4 cup of water and gradually add to the meat mixture. Stir until mixture thickens and boils.

Serve over cooked rice or cooked noodles.

Makes 4 to 6 servings.

****

Cheese Sauce

A while back, as I worked around the kitchen one morning, I was listening to a television station out of the Twin Cities. The television show host was interviewing a woman who owns a fondue restaurant.

"If you want smooth cheese sauce, sprinkle some flour on the shredded cheese before you melt it," she said.

Now—maybe other people already know this, but I didn't. I decided to give it a try, and boy, it worked like a charm.

Use this cheese sauce for homemade Macaroni and Cheese or for whatever else you like to cover with cheese sauce, such as eggs or mashed or baked potatoes.

2 cups shredded medium sharp or sharp cheddar
1 cup milk
2 tablespoons butter
1/4 cup flour

Pour milk into a saucepan and add the butter. Shred the cheddar cheese and put it into a mixing bowl. Mix 1/4 cup flour with it, using a fork to stir it up well so the cheese is coated. Heat the milk and butter until the butter melts. Sprinkle the floured cheese over the milk and butter in the saucepan. Cook over medium heat and continue stirring until the cheese is melted and the sauce has thickened.

Note: a single recipe makes enough for about four cups of cooked noodles.

****

Chicken Paprika

This was one of my dad's favorite recipes for chicken. Unfortunately, I cannot make it nowadays because my husband is allergic to paprika. Do you know how many products contain paprika as a coloring additive?

4 to 6 chicken breasts
1/2 cup flour
1/2 teaspoon salt
1 1/2 teaspoons paprika
1 cup of chopped onion
1 cup tomato puree (or 1 10-ounce can)
1 cup sour cream

Wash chicken. Mix the flour, salt and 1 teaspoon of paprika. Melt a couple of tablespoons of shortening in a heavy skillet. Roll the chicken in the flour and paprika mixture. Place the chicken breasts in the pan, skin side down. Cook until browned (about 15 to 20 minutes). Remove the chicken and set aside.

Add the onion to the skillet and cook and stir until tender. Stir in the tomato puree, another 1/2 teaspoon salt if desired and the 1/2 teaspoon paprika. Add the chicken to the tomato mixture, cover the pan, and cook over medium-low to medium heat until the chicken is tender (30 to 40 minutes or so). Check to make sure the chicken is not sticking from time to time. If it is, stir in a 1/4 cup of water as necessary.

When the chicken breasts are tender, remove from the pan and set aside on a plate. Stir 1 cup of sour cream into the tomato mixture. Heat through. Put the chicken back in the pan and spoon the tomato and sour cream mixture over the chicken.

This is good served with buttered noodles.

****

Chicken and Stuffing Casserole

This recipe is both easy and delicious. I'm normally not all that crazy about stuffing, but this is good. It's also a good way to use leftover chicken or leftover turkey.

2 cups boiling water
1/4 cup butter
4 cups of instant stuffing mix (such as Stove Top or another brand)
4 skinless, boneless chicken breast halves (or you can also use four small chicken breasts)
1 can of cream of mushroom, golden mushroom or cream of celery soup
2/3 soup can of milk

Heat the water to boiling, add the butter and stir until melted. Add the stuffing mix and stir.

Spoon the stuffing mix into a greased casserole dish large enough to hold the stuffing and the chicken (or a 9x13 baking dish).

Arrange the chicken breasts on top of the stuffing. Mix the cream soup and the milk and pour over the chicken breasts and stuffing.

Cover and bake at 350 degrees Fahrenheit for 1 hour or until the chicken breasts are tender. If you are using boneless, skinless chicken breast halves, bake for 45 minutes or until chicken is done. If you are using leftover chicken or turkey, bake at 350 degrees until everything is heated through (30 minutes or so).

✱✱✱✱✱✱✱✱✱✱✱✱✱✱✱✱✱✱✱✱

Corn Chowder
(Easy Recipe)

This easy-to-make soup is especially good on a cold winter day when the wind is howling, the snow is falling, and you would really like nothing better than to stay inside where it's warm! It was one of my mother's favorites because it was a good way to use up some of the corn she had put in the freezer the previous summer.

3 or 4 strips of bacon (or more, if you really like the taste of bacon)
3 medium potatoes
1 medium onion
2 cans of corn
1/2 to 1 cup milk
1/4 cup flour

Cut the bacon into small pieces and fry until almost crisp. Add the onion and fry until cooked through. (I cook the bacon and the onion in the pot that I'm going to make the soup in.)

Cut the potatoes into small pieces. Add to the pot with the bacon and onion. Add just enough water to cover the potatoes. Simmer until the potatoes are tender.

Add the 2 cans of corn. Simmer for a few minutes. Add 1/2 to 1 cup of milk (enough to make the soup the desired consistency).

Mix 1/4 cup flour into a half cup of water and stir until smooth. Pour into the soup and bring to a boil—just long enough to thicken the soup. Add salt and pepper to taste. Serve with crackers or homemade bread.

****

Corn-y Casserole

Instead of cream style corn, you can also use frozen corn or regular canned corn. If you use frozen or canned corn, add 1/2 cup of milk to the recipe. (You do not need to drain the corn, first.)

3 cups dry noodles
3 eggs (beaten)
2 cans cream style corn
1/4 cup butter
1/4 cup chopped onion
1 cup shredded cheddar cheese

Cook and drain noodles. Pour into a large greased casserole dish. Add the butter and stir until melted. Add the beaten eggs, corn, onion and cheese. Mix thoroughly. Bake at 350 degrees Fahrenheit (covered) for 45 minutes or until the noodles are tender and liquid is absorbed.

****

Country-Style Barbecued Ribs

My husband loves Country-Style Barbecued Ribs. I don't care for ordinary barbecued ribs myself, but these are good. Especially if you choose the country-style ribs carefully and buy ribs with more meat than fat.

1 large onion (chopped)
1/2 cup molasses
1/2 cup water
1/4 cup prepared mustard (yellow mustard or horseradish mustard)
2 teaspoons salad oil
1 cup ketchup
1/2 teaspoon salt
3 pounds of country-style ribs

Sauté onion in oil. Add molasses, water, mustard, ketchup and salt. Cook for 10 minutes.

Place ribs in a shallow baking dish or a cake pan. Pour barbecue sauce over ribs. Cover lightly with aluminum foil. Bake at 350 degrees Fahrenheit for 1 1/2 to 2 hours or until the country style ribs are tender.

****

Crispy Baked Chicken

In this recipe, brushing mayonnaise on the chicken after the coating has been baked for a bit is somewhat like frying the chicken, seeing as mayonnaise contains oil. The chicken won't be as greasy as fried chicken, though.

2 cups dried bread crumbs (you can also use crushed corn flakes or wheat flakes cereal)
1/2 teaspoon onion salt
1/4 teaspoon garlic salt
1/4 teaspoon pepper
1/4 teaspoon curry powder (if desired)
4 chicken breasts
3/4 cup mayonnaise

Measure the bread crumbs (or crushed cereal) and seasonings into a mixing bowl and stir until thoroughly combined. Roll the pieces of chicken in the bread crumb mixture and place in a baking pan, skin side up.

Bake at 400 degrees Fahrenheit for 20 minutes.

Remove from the oven and brush the chicken with mayonnaise.

Turn down the oven to 300 degrees Fahrenheit. Return the chicken to the oven and bake 1 to 1 1/2 hours until the chicken is golden and tender when pierced with a fork or sharp knife.

****

1-2-3 Stroganoff

This easy version of stroganoff is as easy as one-two-three. It's a great way to use stew meat. You can also use tougher cuts of steak cut up into small pieces.

> **1 pound of stew meat**
> **1 tablespoon soy sauce**
> **1/2 to 1 can of black olives (depending upon how well you like black olives)**
> **1 medium onion**
> **1 to 2 teaspoons dried basil**
> **1 to 1 1/2 cups sour cream**
> **4 cups cooked noodles**

Brown the stew meat and onion in canola oil or olive oil. Add soy sauce, basil and olives. Stir in the four cups cooked noodles. Stir in the sour cream. Mix thoroughly and heat through.

If the stroganoff seems too dry, add milk in quarter cup increments until it reaches the desired consistency (or use some of the olive juice from the can or add a little more sour cream).

Serve with Parmesan cheese sprinkled on top, if desired, and a salad on the side.

****

Easy-Cheesy Casserole

An easy variation on the old mac-n-cheese standby. Casseroles were a staple for supper when I was growing up on the farm. Casseroles were also a staple when the church ladies served a lunch after a funeral.

1 pound of browned hamburger
1 small to medium onion chopped (if desired)
1 1/2 cups of grated cheddar cheese
4 cups cooked macaroni (or egg noodles; I prefer to use egg noodles myself)
1 can cream of mushroom soup
1/2 soup can of milk
Parmesan cheese to sprinkle on top

Brown hamburger and the onion over medium heat. Cook the macaroni or noodles. Combine hamburger and the pasta in a large baking dish. Add cream of mushroom soup and milk and mix well. Stir in cheddar cheese. Sprinkle Parmesan cheese on top. Cover the casserole dish. Bake in 350 degree Fahrenheit oven for 30 minutes.

* * * * * * * * * * * * * * * * * * * *

Fish Fritters

My husband, father-in-law and brothers-in-law catch quite a few pan fish when they go fishing. They clean the fish and then freeze them in quart freezer bags. Frying the tiny, little individual fillets is a real chore. This recipe is perfect for small fillets such as Bluegill or other sunfish.

3 to 4 cups of fish or small fish fillets (a quart freezer bag)
2 cups of flour
1 teaspoon baking powder
1 teaspoon salt
2 eggs
1 to 1 1/4 cups milk

Measure flour, baking powder, salt, eggs and milk into a medium mixing bowl and stir together until smooth. Add the fish. Stir to coat the fillets with batter.

Heat several inches of oil in a heavy skillet over medium to medium-high heat. Place the fish batter in hot oil by spoonfuls (not the individual fillets but several fillets in a spoonful). Fry until golden brown (5 to 10 minutes each side).

When one batch of fritters is finished, place them on a plate on several layers of paper towel and place the plate in a warm oven to keep the fritters hot until you are ready to serve them. Serve with tartar sauce.

Homemade tartar sauce: 1 cup mayonnaise; several tablespoons of sweet pickle relish; ketchup to taste (several tablespoons). Stir until thoroughly combined.

****

Hash Browned Potatoes

These Hash Browns are made up ahead of time and frozen. The following ingredients make enough for one "skillet" of Hash Browns. Multiply the recipe for as many packages of Hash Browns as you want to freeze.

4 cups of grated boiled potatoes (you can figure about 1 cup per large potato; or 1 cup for 2 smaller potatoes)
1/2 teaspoon salt

1/4 cup vegetable oil
1/4 cup butter

Peel the potatoes. Cook until barely tender. Drain. Cool. Grate the potatoes. Line a skillet with heavy aluminum foil. Use enough aluminum foil to bring up over the sides of the pan.

Measure the potatoes into a mixing bowl. Add the salt. Stir thoroughly.

Pack the potato mixture into the frying pan. Fold the aluminum foil over the potatoes. Remove from the pan. Place in the freezer.

To cook:
Heat the butter and vegetable oil in a heavy skillet over medium to medium-high heat. Carefully remove the aluminum foil (so you don't end up with bits of aluminum foil in your potatoes) and put the circle of frozen Hash Browns into the pan. Cover the skillet. Cook for about five minutes and then remove the cover. Cook for another 10 minutes until the potatoes are browned on the bottom. Cut into wedges and turn. Or, if you think you can manage to turn the potatoes without breaking up the Hash Browns, turn in one piece. Cook another 10 minutes or so until brown on the other side.

****

Homemade Dumpling Noodles
(Egg Noodles)

I like to think of these as "dumpling noodles" because they end up rather thick and chewy and remind me of dumplings. These noodles fill you up and "stick to your ribs." In the "good old days" before macaroni or noodles or pasta of any kind was widely available, this is how my mother said she used to make noodles.

1 to 2 cups flour
2 egg yolks
1 whole egg
1/2 teaspoon salt
1/4 to 1/2 cup water

Measure 1 cup of flour into a mixing bowl. Make a hole in the center of the flour. Add the egg yolks and egg to the hole. Add salt. Mix thoroughly. (A fork works well to mix.)

Add the 1/4 cup water one tablespoon at a time and mix in thoroughly. If the dough seems much too dry, add more water, one tablespoon at a time until the dough is stiff but not crumbly.

Roll out the dough on a well-floured surface. Add more flour to the surface as you go, if necessary. Roll the dough out as thin as you can get it without tearing it.

Use a sharp knife and slice the dough into thin strips about as wide as a pencil. (If you like REALLY WIDE noodles, make the strips a little wider.)

Place the strips of dough on a clean surface and allow them to dry for two hours before cooking.

If you are not going to use the noodles right away and want to store them in an airtight container (up to a month), let the noodles dry for 24 to 48 hours.

To cook the noodles, bring a pot of water to a boil and drop the noodles in one at a time. Cook for 10 or 12 minutes (until tender).

These noodles work well in soup or stew. I have also used them to make macaroni-and-cheese.

Yields about 6 cups of cooked noodles (depending on how thin you roll the dough and how thick you cut the noodles).

****

Homemade Tartar Sauce

I don't know how it is at other houses, but when I make fish, as far as my husband is concerned, fish needs a large amount of tartar sauce. For a lighter version, use fat-free mayonnaise. My sister-in-law makes an excellent sweet pickle relish that I use in the tartar sauce.

1 cup mayonnaise
1/2 cup sweet pickle relish
1/4 cup catsup

Measure all ingredients into a bowl and mix thoroughly. Any leftover tartar sauce will keep in the refrigerator for several weeks. Add more mayonnaise or pickle relish or catsup to taste.

Yield: 1 3/4 cups of tartar sauce

****

Homemade Pizza Crust
(Thick crust)

This recipe for pizza crust makes dough that's easy to roll out. Occasionally I will make a frozen pizza I bought at the store and will add extra meat and cheese. When we're finished eating, my husband says, "Well, that was a nice start. What's next?" When I make this recipe for homemade pizza, my husband eats all he wants and there are still leftovers that he can take to work the next day for lunch. With the olive oil or canola oil and the oatmeal, this pizza crust is heart-healthy, too.

> **3 cups of flour (if you want, use 2 cups of white flour and 1 cup of whole wheat)**
> **1 package of dry yeast (or 2 teaspoons of bulk yeast)**
> **1/2 teaspoon salt**
> **1 cup warm water**
> **1/2 cup of olive oil or canola oil**
> **1 cup of dry oatmeal**
> **1 to 2 teaspoons of basil or dry Italian seasoning mix (optional)**
> **1/4 to 1/2 teaspoon Lemon pepper seasoning (optional)**

Pour the water into a mixing bowl. Add yeast. Stir until the yeast dissolves. Add the salt, olive oil or canola oil and oatmeal. If you want, stir in 1 or 2 teaspoons of basil or dry Italian seasoning mix and/or 1/4 to 1/2 teaspoon of lemon pepper seasoning. Mix until thoroughly combined. Knead the dough for a minute or two.

Roll out the dough to fit your pizza pan. Or you can use a jelly roll pan.

Spread a layer of spaghetti sauce over the dough. Add your favorite ingredients: sliced black olives, chopped onion, chopped green pepper, hamburger (brown it first and drain), pepperoni, diced ham, Canadian bacon, diced summer sausage—whatever you like. Top with 2 to 3 cups of shredded mozzarella cheese and 1 cup of cheddar cheese (if desired).

Bake at 375 degrees Fahrenheit for 25 to 30 minutes. Allow to cool for 5 minutes before cutting and serving.

****

Homemade Thin Pizza Crust

This recipe mixes up in just a few minutes. Using olive oil, for some reason, seems to make the dough roll out easier.

2 cups flour (1 cup of white flour and 1 cup of whole wheat flour, if desired)
1 teaspoon baking powder
1/4 teaspoon salt
2/3 cup warm water
1/4 cup Olive oil
1 to 2 teaspoons of basil or dry Italian seasoning mix (optional)
1/4 to 1/2 teaspoon lemon pepper seasoning (optional)

Measure all ingredients into a mixing bowl and stir until the dough is formed. Place the dough on a floured surface and knead for a minute or so.

Roll out the dough to fit your pizza pan. Or you can use a jelly roll pan.

Spread a layer of spaghetti sauce over the dough. Add your favorite ingredients: sliced black olives, chopped onion, chopped green pepper, hamburger (brown it first and drain), pepperoni, diced ham, Canadian bacon, diced summer sausage—whatever you like. Top with 2 to 3 cups of shredded mozzarella cheese or a combination of mozzarella and cheddar cheese.

Bake at 375 degrees Fahrenheit for 25 to 30 minutes. Allow to cool for 5 minutes before cutting and serving.

****

Hot German Potato Salad

My father's mother was from Germany, and Dad loved Hot German Potato Salad (which is not what I would consider salad, seeing as it is served hot). Unfortunately, my grandmother died long before I was born so I never had a chance to know her. Interestingly enough, however, even though my mother was Norwegian, she liked Hot German Potato Salad too. And so do I!

potatoes (6 to 8 medium)
4 slices bacon
1/2 cup chopped onion
2 tablespoons flour
2 tablespoons sugar
1/2 teaspoon salt
1/2 teaspoon celery seed
3/4 cup water
1/4 cup vinegar

Peel the potatoes and cut into small pieces (I cut the potatoes in 1/2 inch slices and cut the slices into fourths). Cover with water, add 1/2 teaspoon salt and boil until tender. When the potatoes are done, drain off the water and set them aside.

Cut the four slices of bacon into small pieces and place in a large skillet. Add the chopped onion. Fry over medium heat until the bacon is crisp and the onion is tender. Stir in the flour, sugar, salt and celery seed. Cook until bubbly, stirring constantly. Stir in the water and vinegar. Cook for about a minute until the mixture thickens, stirring constantly.

Add the potatoes to the mixture in the skillet and stir to coat the potatoes. Serve hot. Makes four to six servings. Hot German Potato salad is especially good with pork chops. It makes a nice side dish for meatloaf or roast, too.

****

Kangaroo Pouches
(Hot Sandwiches)

The recipe makes approximately 15 or 16 sandwiches. Leftovers can be used for snacks and to take to work for lunch. My husband is especially fond of these and loves to heat them up in the microwave at work for his lunch.

Sandwich Pouches:
    1 1/2 cups warm water
    1 package dry yeast (or 2 teaspoons bulk yeast)
    1/3 cup canola oil
    1/2 teaspoon salt
    1/2 cup dry oatmeal
    4 1/2 to 5 cups flour

Dissolve yeast in warm water. Stir in remaining ingredients. Knead for a couple of minutes. Dough will be a little soft and sticky. Divide dough into balls the size of small eggs.

Filling:
Use what you like for the filling. I have included slices of summer sausage, thin-sliced ham, cotto salami, smoked turkey breast, dried beef. For the cheese, I have used cheddar, Colby, and mozzarella.

Assembling the Kangaroo Pouches:
Roll dough to approximately 6 inches wide by 8 inches long. Place a slice of meat and a slice of cheese slightly below the center of the dough. Drizzle a few drops of Italian salad dressing or a scant teaspoon of spaghetti sauce over the cheese. I have also used a scant teaspoon of sour cream or blue cheese salad dressing. Bring the top part of the dough over the filling and seal the edges by rolling up the dough toward the filling. Place sandwiches on a greased baking sheet.

Bake at 325 degrees for 20 to 25 minutes. Some of the cheese may melt out of the Kangaroo Pouches, but in that case, when you serve them, scoop the melted cheese on top of the sandwiches. Serve with a salad or other fresh vegetables.

Note: since two cookie sheets will not fit side-by-side in my oven, I make up the first cookie sheet of sandwiches, and while they are baking, I make up the second cookie sheet of sandwiches.

Electric skillet: I have also baked these in a non-stick electric skillet. Cook on each side for approximately 10 minutes at 325 degrees Fahrenheit.

* * * * * * * * * * * * * * * * * * * *

Lasagna Casserole

This recipe makes a large dish of lasagna casserole. If you only have a couple of people to eat it, consider freezing some of it.

6 cups of egg noodles cooked
1 jar or can of spaghetti sauce
1 pound of hamburger browned
1 cup sour cream
4 ounces cream cheese
3 cups grated cheddar cheese
1 cup sliced black olives (optional)
1 medium onion chopped (optional)

While hamburger is browning (with chopped onion if desired), cook the egg noodles. Add the spaghetti sauce, sour cream, cream cheese and 2 cups of cheddar cheese to the hamburger and stir until thoroughly combined. Add the cooked egg noodles. Add the sliced black olives (if desired). Stir until thoroughly combined. Spoon the mixture into a casserole dish. Sprinkle 1 cup of cheddar cheese on the top. Cover.

Bake at 350 degrees Fahrenheit for 1 hour. Serve with garlic bread (or garlic breadsticks) and a salad, if desired.

****

Meat Loaf

Meat loaf, scalloped potatoes and a vegetable, such as green beans, carrots or sweet corn, was often on the menu for supper at our house when I was a kid growing up on the farm. Since it was hard for my mother to get around because of the polio paralysis, she could put this supper together and let the oven do the rest of the work.

1 1/2 to 2 pounds hamburger
1 cup cracker crumbs
1/2 cup milk
1 egg
1 small onion, chopped
1/2 teaspoon salt
1/4 to 1/2 teaspoon ground mustard or 1 to 2 tablespoons prepared mustard (if desired)
1/2 teaspoon of dry basil (if desired)
1/4 teaspoon garlic powder (if desired)
catsup (if desired)

Crush the crackers and put them in a mixing bowl. Add the milk. Add the chopped onion. Let stand for a few minutes. Add the egg, salt, hamburger and any seasonings that you want to include. Mix with your hands until thoroughly combined.

Spoon into an ungreased loaf pan.

Bake at 350 degrees Fahrenheit for 1 1/2 hours. Half an hour before the meat loaf is finished, spread catsup over the top and let the meat loaf finished baking (if desired). Personally, I prefer to put the catsup on my meat loaf just before I eat it!

****

Norma's Scalloped Potatoes

Since my mother could not get around very well because of the polio, she really liked this recipe because it is easy.

6 to 8 medium potatoes
2 cans Golden Mushroom soup
 or
2 cans Cream of Chicken soup
1 1/2 soup cans milk (if you're using more potatoes, use 2 soup cans of milk)

Peel the potatoes and cut into fairly thin slices. Put the soup into a mixing bowl, add the milk, and use a whisk or an electric mixer to stir together until smooth. (**Note:** if I am using potatoes that have a nice, clean, unblemished peeling, sometimes I scrub them up with a scrub brush under running water and do not peel potatoes.)

Grease a casserole dish, and put a layer of potato slices in the bottom. Pour some of the soup mixture over the potatoes. Add another layer of potatoes and more soup. Continue until all of the potatoes are in the casserole. Save some of the soup mixture to pour over the top.

Bake covered in a 350 degree Fahrenheit oven for 1 1/2 hours (or until potatoes are tender). Let stand for 5 to 10 minutes before serving.

****

Norwegian Meatballs and Gravy

I am calling this recipe "Norwegian Meatballs and Gravy" because this is how my mother made meatballs and gravy. My mother generally used milk when she made any kind of gravy, except for turkey gravy at Thanksgiving, but my sister usually made the gravy for Thanksgiving. Adding nutmeg to the meatballs is a "Norwegian" thing to do.

1/2 cup chopped onion
1 1/2 to 2 pounds ground beef
1/2 cup dry bread crumbs (or crushed saltine crackers)
1/4 cup milk
1 egg
1/2 to 1 teaspoon salt (if you use salted saltine crackers, use 1/2 teaspoon of salt, unless you like really salty meatballs)
1/4 teaspoon pepper
1/2 teaspoon nutmeg

Measure the bread crumbs or cracker crumbs into a mixing bowl. Pour the milk over the crumbs and let sit for a few minutes. Beat in the egg. Add the ground beef, onion, salt, pepper and nutmeg. Mix until thoroughly combined. (I use my hands for this process.)

Melt a few tablespoons of shortening into a skillet. Make the meatballs about the size of a small egg. Fry in the shortening over medium heat until browned and the meatballs are cooked through (about 20 minutes or so, depending on how big you make your meatballs). Turn several times while cooking. Cover the pan in between turning the meatballs.

To make gravy:
Remove the meatballs and set aside. Melt a quarter cup of butter in the pan and stir into the meat drippings. Add a quarter cup of flour. Stir into the butter and meat drippings and cook over medium heat until bubbly. Slowly pour 2 cups of milk into the pan, stirring while you pour. Stir constantly and cook until the gravy thickens. If the gravy seems too thick, add milk by the tablespoon and cook until it reaches desired consistency. Add salt to taste.

Add the meatballs to the gravy and stir gently until the meatballs are coated. Heat through.

Serve with mashed potatoes. Or if you would rather—serve over cooked egg noodles or brown rice.

****

Onion and Mushroom Soup

My husband loves this soup served with grilled cheese sandwiches. I like the recipe because it's a quick and easy way to make homemade soup!

2 medium onions or 1 very large onion
1 pound of fresh mushrooms (or 2 8-ounce cans of mushrooms)
1/4 cup butter
3 cups water
3 teaspoons beef bouillon granules
1/4 cup burgundy wine (or cranberry juice or grape juice) (optional)

Peel the onions, cut into slices and separate into rings. Wash the mushrooms. Cut into slices. Melt the butter in a large skillet. Sauté the onions and mushrooms until the onions and mushrooms have softened.

If you are using canned mushrooms, sauté the onions until softened and then add the cans of mushrooms (you do not need to drain the mushrooms). Add the water. Stir in the beef bouillon granules. Stir in the wine or cranberry juice. Simmer for 10 to 15 minutes.

Serve with croutons and shredded cheddar cheese sprinkled on top, if desired.

****

Oven Fried (Baked) Potatoes & Fish

This recipe takes about 30 minutes from start to finish. The hardest work is scrubbing the potatoes.

Preheat oven to 400 degrees Fahrenheit

Scrub 3 or 4 medium potatoes and slice into 1/4 inch thick slices

Coat the bottom of a 9x13 pan with canola oil or olive oil

Place potato slices in a bowl. Drizzle 1 tablespoon of canola oil or olive oil over potatoes. Sprinkle with dried basil (or use another seasoning if you prefer, such as garlic powder or lemon pepper) and salt to taste. Mix well.

Arrange slices in the 9x13 pan. Bake at 400 degrees for 10 minutes. Turn potato slices over and bake for another 10 to 15 minutes or until slightly crispy and cooked through.

These potatoes go well with baked fish. Put the fish in the oven for the second half of baking time for the potatoes. The fish and potatoes will be done at the same time.

To oven bake fish: coat another 9x13 pan with canola oil or olive oil. Arrange fish fillets in the pan. Turn over after 5 minutes and bake the other side for another 5 minutes. Serve with tartar sauce, lemon slices and/or melted butter.

****

Onion Potato Bake

This recipe is contains the basic ingredients for potato pancakes, but the mixture is baked in a casserole dish.

2 eggs (beaten)
1/4 cup flour
1/2 teaspoon baking powder
1 teaspoon salt
1/2 cup chopped onion
8 medium potatoes (shredded)
1/2 cup melted butter
paprika (if desired)

Use an electric mixer to beat the eggs, flour, baking powder and salt together. Stir in onions, potatoes and butter. Mix well.

Spoon mixture into a greased casserole dish. Sprinkle with paprika (if desired). Cover the casserole dish and bake at 350 degrees Fahrenheit for one hour or until the potatoes are tender and the top is crisp and brown.

****

Pot Roast

We quite often had pot roast for Sunday dinner when I was growing up on the farm. Sunday dinner was a *special occasion,* and before we went to church, my mother or sister would put a pot roast in the oven. There was nothing like coming home to the smell of pot roast and knowing how good it was going to taste when dinnertime finally arrived.

4 or 5 pound pot roast
6 medium potatoes (peeled)
6 to 8 carrots (peeled and cut in quarters)
1 medium onion

Place the pot roast in a casserole dish or baking pan large enough to hold it. Sprinkle the top side of the roast with salt. Cut the onions into slices and lay across the top of the roast. Arrange the potatoes and carrots around the roast. Cover the casserole dish.

Bake at 300 degrees Fahrenheit for 3 to 4 hours—until the vegetables and the roast are tender.

Remove the roast from the oven. Put the potatoes in a serving dish and place back in the warm oven. Put the carrots in a serving dish and place back in the warm oven. Put the roast on a serving plate and place back in the warm oven.

Gravy:

Skim the fat off the broth base remaining in the casserole dish or baking pan.

Pour the broth into a measuring cup. Add enough water to make 2 cups. Add 1 to 2 teaspoons of beef bouillon granules, if desired.

Put a quarter cup of water into a small bowl and make a paste by adding a 1/2 cup of flour. When the paste is smooth, stir in another quarter cup of water.

Put the broth into a saucepan and slowly stir in the flour mixture. Cook over medium heat until thickened.

****

Potato Pancakes

My husband loves these with venison steak (or any kind of steak) or sliced ham and/or with eggs. As far as I'm concerned, they make a meal in and of themselves.

6 to 8 medium potatoes
1 egg
1 small onion (chopped)
1/4 cup flour
1/2 teaspoon salt

Peel the potatoes and shred. Beat the egg with a fork in a separate bowl and pour over the potatoes. Mix in the onion, flour and salt.

Melt 1 or 2 tablespoons of shortening in a frying pan (I always use my electric fry pan because I can get all of the pancakes in there at once).

Spoon the potato mixture into the fry pan by large spoonfuls. Press down with the back of the spoon. Cook over medium heat, approximately eight minutes on each side, until golden brown.

This recipe makes between six and eight potato pancakes, depending upon the size of the spoonfuls of the potato mixture.

****

Potato Soup
(with cheddar cheese and sour cream)

When I was a little girl, my mother would tell me that when she was a girl, potato soup was often what they ate for their evening meal. My grandfather raised potatoes to sell, so they always had potatoes. And since they also had milk cows, they always had milk, too.

3 to 4 medium to large potatoes
2 to 3 medium carrots
1/2 cup chopped onion
1/2 teaspoon salt
1 cup milk
1 cup shredded cheddar cheese (I have also used mozzarella)
1/2 cup sour cream
2 to 3 tablespoons butter

Peel the potatoes and the carrots. Cut into small pieces. Put into a soup pot and cover with water. Add 1/2 teaspoon of salt. Boil until the potatoes and carrots are tender. A few minutes before the potatoes and carrots are done, add the onion.

When the potatoes and carrots are cooked, add 1 cup of milk and 2 to 3 tablespoons of butter. (Do not drain the liquid off the pot when the carrots and potatoes are finished cooking.) Heat through. Add shredded cheese. Continue stirring over low heat until the cheese is melted. Add the sour cream. Stir over low heat until the sour cream has been mixed in completely.

Makes 4 to 6 servings.

****

Potato Wedges

These go by different names in restaurants (Texas fries and whatnot), but I just call them "potato wedges." They are especially good with hamburgers or chicken or steak.

1 medium potato per serving
Canola oil

Microwave the potato or potatoes until they are nearly cooked but are still firm. (You can also use leftover baked potatoes.)

Allow the potatoes to cool for several minutes so you can handle them without burning your fingers. Cut the potatoes into quarters and then cut the quarters lengthwise into slices.

Fill a small saucepan half full with Canola oil. Or put an inch or two of oil in a medium frying pan. Heat oil over medium high heat until it is hot enough to fry the potatoes. Cook in the Canola oil until crispy and golden brown. Turn several times while cooking, being careful not to splash hot oil. Place on paper towels to drain off excess oil. If you are making several servings of potato wedges, put them in the oven at 200 degree Fahrenheit to keep them hot until you are ready to serve. Sprinkle with salt, if desired, before serving.

Alternate method: Coat the potatoes with Canola oil or olive oil, place on a baking sheet and bake in the oven at 400 degrees Fahrenheit for 20 minutes (or until crispy and golden brown). Turn several times while baking.

****

Savory Rice

This makes a good side dish with chicken or pork chops—or whatever else you're having for supper.

6 tablespoons butter
1 medium onion chopped
1 1/2 cups uncooked rice (I like to use brown rice)
1/2 teaspoon ground allspice
1/2 teaspoon turmeric
1/4 teaspoon of curry powder (I leave out the curry powder because my husband, Randy, doesn't care for it)
3 1/2 cups of chicken bullion broth—or if you're serving pork or beef, use beef bullion
1 cup of slivered almonds (if desired)

Melt the butter in a heavy skillet. Add the onion and uncooked rice. Cook over medium heat until the onion is browned, stirring constantly. Add the seasonings. Stir thoroughly.

Grease a large casserole dish (2 quart or larger). Spoon the rice and onion mixture into the casserole dish. Heat the broth to boiling and pour over the rice mixture. Stir.

Put a cover on the casserole dish and bake at 350 degrees Fahrenheit for 30 to 40 minutes until all of the liquid is absorbed. Before serving, stir in the almonds.

Makes about six servings.

****

Sunday Dinner (Chicken or Pork Chops)

You can use either chicken or pork chops in this recipe.

1 1/2 cups of uncooked rice (white or brown) (I like to use brown rice. You can also mix in some wild rice with the brown or white rice, if you want.)
4 pieces of chicken or 4 pork chops
1/4 to 1/2 package of onion soup mix
1 can of cream of chicken soup or cream of mushroom soup or golden mushroom soup
1 can of milk
1/2 can of water

Grease a casserole dish large enough to hold the chicken or pork chops and rice. Place uncooked rice in the bottom of the casserole.

Arrange the pork chops or the chicken in the casserole dish on top of the rice. Sprinkle some of the onion soup mix over the meat.

Open the can of soup and dump into a small mixing bowl. Add the can of milk and the half a can of water. Stir until smooth with a fork or a whisk. Pour over the chicken or the pork chops. Cover. Bake for about 2 hours at 325 degrees Fahrenheit (or until the chicken or pork chops are tender and the rice is cooked).

****

Sweet and Sour Chicken

This is another easy way to cook chicken with a short preparation time. Serve with rice or Savory Rice. That way, your oven can be working double duty. To bake plain rice in the oven, use the same proportions as when you boil rice (1 cup of rice to 2 cups of water). Put the rice and water in a casserole dish. Add a tablespoon of butter or olive oil. Stir once while the rice is baking (after the butter has melted). Remove the rice from the oven when all of the liquid has been absorbed. The rice and chicken should finish up at about the same time.

8 ounces Western salad dressing (or French dressing or any salad dressing with a tomato base)
1 package of dry onion soup mix (If you don't want as much salt, use a half a package.)
8 ounces of apricot preserves or any other kind of jam or jelly that you prefer
1/2 cup water
6 to 8 chicken breasts

Mix salad dressing, soup mix and jam/jelly with 1/2 cup water.

Place chicken in a baking dish. Pour sauce over chicken pieces. Cover baking dish. Bake at 350 degrees Fahrenheit for 1 to 1 1/2 hours (until chicken is tender).

Note: You can use apricot juice instead of preserves or another juice if you prefer. If you use the juice, then eliminate the 1/2 cup of water.

****

Sweet & Sour
Lemon & Honey Chicken

This was one of my mother's favorite recipes for chicken because it is so easy.

4 chicken breasts
1/2 cup lemon juice
1/4 cup cooking oil (Canola oil, olive oil, whatever you prefer)
2 tablespoons honey
dash of garlic powder or garlic salt (more if you prefer a stronger garlic taste)

In a small saucepan, cook the lemon juice, oil, honey and garlic powder for one minute.

Put the chicken breasts into a greased baking dish. Pour the marinade over the chicken breasts. Cover the casserole dish. Set in the refrigerator for one hour.

Bake the chicken breasts at 350 degrees Fahrenheit for 1 to 1 1/2 hours or until chicken is tender. Baste several times while baking.

Note: if desired, add 1/4 teaspoon of salt to the marinade. My mother never used salt because she suffered from high blood pressure.

****

Sweet and Sour Meatballs

Served over rice, these meatballs are an interesting variation on meatballs with mashed potatoes and gravy.

1 1/2 to 2 pounds of ground beef
1 cup cracker crumbs
1 small onion chopped into small pieces
1 egg
1/4 cup milk
1/2 teaspoon salt
2 heaping tablespoons cornstarch
1/2 cup brown sugar
1 can (about 13 ounces) of pineapple chunks
juice from the pineapple chunks
2 tablespoons vinegar
1 tablespoon corn starch

Dump the ground beef into a mixing bowl and add the cracker crumbs, onion, egg, salt and milk. Use your hands to stir the mixture until thoroughly combined.

Melt a couple of tablespoons of shortening in a heavy skillet and shape the ground beef into small balls. Brown over medium heat. Cover and cook until the meatballs are done.

Remove the meatballs from the pan and set aside.

In a small bowl, mix the cornstarch and the brown sugar. If necessary, add water to the pineapple juice to make 2 cups. Add the pineapple juice/water, vinegar and soy sauce to the cornstarch and brown sugar and stir until smooth.

Pour into the skillet and cook over medium heat until thickened. Add the pineapple chunks. Add the meatballs and heat through.

Serve over hot rice.

****

Swiss Steak

Swiss Steak was one of our regular meals while I was growing up.

2 pounds of round steak
1/4 cup flour
1/2 teaspoon salt (or garlic salt, if desired)
1/4 teaspoon pepper (if desired)
1 medium onion

Mix the flour, salt and pepper. Pour half of the flour mixture on one side of the meat and pound in with a meat hammer. Turn the meat over and pound the rest of the flour mixture into the opposite side.

Melt a couple of tablespoons of shortening in a heavy skillet over medium heat. Cut the round steak into smaller serving pieces. Brown the meat on both sides. Cut the onion into slices and place on top of the meat.

Cover the pan and cook until the meat is tender (up to an hour). You may have to turn the heat down a bit. After 15 minutes or so, check to see if the meat is sticking to the pan. If it is, add 1/4 cup of water. Add more water later as necessary.

If desired, make gravy in the pan when the meat is tender and serve with mashed potatoes or rice.

Gravy:
Remove the meat, put on a plate and set in a warm oven until you are ready to serve.

Melt 2 tablespoons shortening in the pan and stir into the drippings. Add 2 cups of water and one or two teaspoons of beef bouillon granules (if you want a more beefy taste to the gravy).

Put a quarter cup of water into a small bowl and make a paste by adding a 1/2 cup of flour. When the paste is smooth, stir in another quarter cup of water.

Slowly stir in the flour mixture into the mixture in the skillet. Cook over medium heat until thickened.

****

Taco Pie

This is an easy recipe that also allows you to make use of those crumbs that accumulate in the bottom of the taco chip bags! (My husband really loves taco chips, so maybe we end up with more crumbs than your average household…)

1 pound hamburger
1 small onion chopped
taco seasoning or chili seasoning
1 cup sliced black olives
2 cups crushed taco chips
1/2 cup sour cream
1 cup shredded cheddar cheese

Crust:
2 cups flour
3/4 cup of warm water
1 package of dry yeast (or 2 teaspoons bulk yeast)
1/2 teaspoon salt
1/4 cup vegetable oil
1/2 cup dry oatmeal

Filling: Cook hamburger, add onions and add taco seasoning or chili seasoning to taste. Add olives and sour cream. Heat well.

Crust: Dissolve yeast in warm water, add remaining ingredients and roll out to fit a large pie pan. Sprinkle one cup of crushed taco chips over the crust. Add meat mixture. Put remaining taco chips on top of the meat. Sprinkle the shredded cheese on top of the chips. Bake for 20 minutes at 375 degrees Fahrenheit.

Note: If you would rather not use taco seasoning or chili seasoning (due to problems with acid reflux or heartburn), I have used catsup in the recipe. My husband and I laugh about it because in one of those "you know you live in Wisconsin if" things, one of the items is, "you know you live in Wisconsin if you think catsup is just a little too spicy." Norwegians don't seem to care much for really spicy food. My husband is not of Norwegian descent, but I am…

****

Three-Bean Hotdish

My mother and my big sister used to make this quite often while I was growing up on our farm. This has always been one of my favorites! There's just something about the mixture of bean flavors and the hamburger and bacon and onion...

1 (15 ounce or so) can of kidney beans
1 (15 ounce or so) can of lima beans
1 (15 ounce or so) can of baked beans
1 pound of hamburger
1 small to medium onion
1/2 pound of bacon
1/4 to 1/2 cup brown sugar (1/2 cup if you want the hotdish to taste sweeter)
1/2 cup catsup
1 1/2 teaspoons prepared mustard (optional)
1/2 teaspoon salt

Cut the bacon into pieces and brown over medium heat in a heavy skillet. Drain fat from pan. Set aside. Add the onion pieces and the hamburger. Cook over medium heat until the hamburger is browned. Add some of the bacon fat if necessary.

Pour the kidney beans, lima beans and baked beans into a greased casserole. Add the bacon and hamburger mixture. Add the sugar, catsup, mustard and salt. Stir thoroughly to mix together. Bake at 350 degrees Fahrenheit for 45 to 50 minutes.

Note: This is very good served with fresh homemade bread and real butter!

****

Tuna Loaf Casserole

I don't know about others, but when I think of tuna fish, I think of sandwiches. This recipe makes a quick and easy way to serve tuna as a main dish.

12 ounces canned tuna
1/4 cup minced onion
1/4 cup lemon juice
1/4 teaspoon salt
1/4 teaspoon pepper
1/2 teaspoon ground thyme
2 cups coarse cracker crumbs
1/2 cup milk
4 eggs beaten
1 tablespoon olive oil

Drain the cans of tuna. Save the liquid. Put the tuna in a mixing bowl. Add onion, lemon juice, salt, pepper, thyme and cracker crumbs. Mix.

Add the tuna liquid plus enough milk to make 1 cup. Put the eggs into a separate bowl and beat in the olive oil (you don't have to get out the mixer; a fork will do). Pour the milk, eggs and olive oil mixture over the tuna and stir thoroughly. Spoon the tuna mixture into a loaf pan or casserole dish (don't cover the dish). Bake at 350 degrees Fahrenheit for 1 hour or until set in the center.

Allow to cool for 10 minutes before slicing. Serve with a tossed salad or coleslaw.

****

Vegetable Soup

The nice thing about soup, of course, is that you can use what you have available for vegetables and for meat. When I was a kid, vegetable soup was one of our "staple" meals. My mother would use leftover steak or roast to make soup. Homemade vegetable soup is especially good with homemade bread.

1 onion chopped
1/2 pound to 1 pound of sausage links cut into pieces (or ground pork sausage or beef or venison stew meat)
3 medium to large carrots
3 medium to large potatoes
1 turnip (optional)
1 cup of green beans
1 cup of sweet corn
3 to 4 cups water
1/2 teaspoon salt (instead of salt, you can use 1 teaspoon of beef bouillon granules)
1/8 teaspoon dried thyme

Sauté the onion in several tablespoons of butter in a large saucepan or another kettle. Add the sausage slices (or the ground pork sausage or the stew meat) and continue frying and stirring the meat until it is brown and cooked through(or heated through if it is pre-cooked sausage).

Add the water. Heat to boiling. Simmer for 15 minutes. Add the vegetables.

Simmer for 30 minutes to 1 hour.

Serve with crackers or homemade bread and real butter.

****

Cookies
&
Bars

Brown Sugar Drops

Drop cookies are, of course, the easiest of all cookies to make. Brown Sugar Drops are quick and easy way to satisfy my sweet tooth!

1/2 cup butter
1/2 cup shortening
2 cups brown sugar
2 eggs
1/2 cup buttermilk or water (or 1/2 cup of milk with 1 tablespoon of lemon juice or vinegar)
3 1/2 cups flour
1 teaspoon baking soda
1/2 teaspoon salt
1 teaspoon vanilla

Measure the butter, shortening and sugar into a mixing bowl. Cream together. Beat in the eggs. Add the milk (or water), flour, baking soda, vanilla and salt. Mix until thoroughly combined.

Drop dough by teaspoonfuls onto a greased cookie sheet. Bake at 350 degrees Fahrenheit for 10 to 12 minutes (pat a cookie lightly with your forefinger. If no imprint remains, the cookies are done).

Makes about 4 dozen cookies.

****

Brownies

There's nothing like old-fashioned fudge brownies. (I also like to think of them as "anti-oxidant protein bars" because of the eggs and cocoa.) When I need to make something in a hurry for a bake sale or a church event, I like to use this recipe because it is quick and easy. These are especially good made with walnuts—if I have managed to find walnuts on sale.

1/3 cup cocoa (heaping) (or a 1/2 cup if you really want the bars to be dark chocolate)
2/3 cup Canola oil
2 cups of sugar
4 eggs
1 teaspoon salt
1 teaspoon baking powder
1 teaspoon vanilla
1 1/4 cups flour
1 cup of chopped walnuts (optional)

Measure all ingredients into a large mixing bowl. Mix until thoroughly combined, using either an electric mixer or a wire whisk.

Spoon into a greased 9x13 pan. Bake at 350 degrees Fahrenheit for 30 minutes (or until bars have pulled away from the pan slightly).

Cool. Cut. Serve. Enjoy!

****

Butterscotch Brownies

These butterscotch brownies are baked in an 8x8 pan. They are very tasty. Plus, it's a small pan, so I'm not tempted to eat so many!

1/4 cup Canola oil (or another vegetable oil)
1 cup packed brown sugar
1 egg
1 teaspoon of vanilla
1/2 teaspoon salt
3/4 cup flour
1 cup chopped walnuts

Measure the Canola oil, brown sugar, egg, vanilla and salt into a mixing bowl. Beat with a spoon or an electric mixer until smooth. Stir in the flour and walnuts until thoroughly combined.

Spread into a greased 8x8 pan. Bake at 350 degrees Fahrenheit for about 25 minutes or until the brownies are firm when tapped with your finger.

****

Best Ever Chocolate Chip Cookies

If you like soft, chewy chocolate chip cookies, give this recipe a try. When I was growing up on our farm, chocolate chip cookies were one of my big sister's specialties.

2 sticks butter (or 1 stick butter and 1/2 cup shortening)
1 cup brown sugar
2 eggs
1 teaspoon vanilla
1/4 cup water
3 cups flour
1 teaspoon salt
1 1/2 teaspoons baking soda
1 large bag of chocolate chips
1 cup chopped walnuts (optional)

Cream the butter and brown sugar. Beat in the eggs. Add the vanilla, water, baking soda and salt. Stir in the flour. Stir in the chocolate chips and walnuts.

Drop by teaspoonfuls onto a greased cookie sheet. Bake at 350 degrees Fahrenheit for 11 to 12 minutes. Remove from cookie sheet immediately.

****

Chocolate Easter Bunny Cake

To make this double-chocolate Easter bunny cake (chocolate cake and chocolate frosting), use your round layer-cake pan. It's always fun to have an Easter Bunny cake at Easter. I made one for Easter the year my first great-nephew was almost a year old. He got a big kick out of it!

In addition to the cake and frosting, you will need:
**jelly beans
coconut
malted milk eggs (the large ones that come in a variety of colors)
2 wafer cookies (for the ears)
licorice whips for the whiskers (or use regular licorice twists cut lengthwise in pieces several inches long)**

Cake
**1 1/2 cups flour
1 cup sugar
1 teaspoon baking powder
1/2 teaspoon salt
1/3 cup cocoa
3/4 cup milk
1/2 cup cooking oil
1 egg
1 teaspoon vanilla**

Measure all ingredients into a medium-sized bowl. Use an electric mixer and blend at low speed for 1 minute. Scrape the bowl while blending. Beat at high speed for 2 to 3 minutes, scraping the bowl occasionally. Bake at 350 degrees Fahrenheit for 35 to 40 minutes in a greased and floured round layer-cake pan. Allow the cake to cool thoroughly before removing it from the pan.

Frosting
**3 cups powdered sugar
1/4 cup plus 1 tablespoon cocoa
6 tablespoons softened butter**

Measure all ingredients into a medium-sized mixing bowl. Blend at low speed for 1 minute. Scrape the bowl while blending. Beat at high speed for 2 to 3 minutes, scraping occasionally. If frosting seems too stiff, add milk by the teaspoon until the frosting reaches the desired consistency. If the frosting seems too thin, add powdered sugar by the tablespoon until the frosting reaches the desired consistency.

How to Make Your Chocolate Easter Bunny Cake

After the cake has cooled completely, remove from the round cake pan. Cut in half. Frost the flat side of one half and put the two pieces together (so they look like a half moon). Place on a platter or a large plate, cut side down so the half circle is upright (not laying flat).

Frost the cake with chocolate frosting.

Place two jelly beans for the eyes and one jelly bean for the nose. Use a large malted milk egg for the tail. Stick the pieces of licorice into the frosting/cake on both sides of the nose for whiskers.

With a sharp knife, cut a hole on each side of the head toward the top where you want to place the ears. To make the ears, use the sharp knife to trim a wafer cookie into the shape of bunny ears. You may have to try several times before you get wafer cookies that look like ears. I have to, anyway, because I usually end up breaking the cookies before I am finished! Frost the ears. Put a little frosting into the holes to anchor the ears.

Sprinkle coconut around the Easter bunny cake. Decorate the coconut with jelly beans and malted milk eggs.

****

Chocolate Chip Peanut Butter Bars

These bars are one of my favorites. Chocolate *and* peanut butter. Yum!

**1/2 cup butter
1/2 cup shortening
1 cup white sugar
1 cup brown sugar (packed)
1 cup peanut butter
2 eggs
2 teaspoons vanilla
3 cups flour
1 teaspoon soda
1/2 teaspoon salt
1 cup chopped walnuts
1 twelve-ounce package of chocolate chips (or 2 six-ounce packages)**

Measure the shortening, butter, white sugar and brown sugar into a mixing bowl. Cream together. Stir in the peanut butter. Beat in the eggs. Add the vanilla, baking soda and salt. Add the flour and walnuts. Stir until thoroughly combined.

Spoon batter into a greased 9x13 pan. Bake at 350 degrees Fahrenheit for 30 to 35 minutes (until bars feel set when you tap them with your finger). Try not to over bake, otherwise the bars end up dry.

****

Christmas Cookies

These cookies are good at any time, but they are especially festive at Christmas because they contain spices, dried fruit and chopped walnuts.

1/2 cup butter
1/2 cup shortening
3 cups brown sugar
4 eggs
1 cup milk
1/2 teaspoon salt
2 teaspoons baking powder
1/2 teaspoon ground cloves
1/2 teaspoon ground cinnamon
1/2 teaspoon ground nutmeg
1 cup citron (For those who are not familiar with it, Citron is a type of candied melon rind that comes in a package of different colored pieces — red, green, white. The mixture also is sometimes called "fruitcake mix" or "holiday mix." If you cannot find anything similar in your grocery store, you can substitute chopped green and red candied cherries. You could also use golden raisins.)
1 cup dark raisins
2 cups chopped walnuts
4 1/2 cups flour

Measure the butter, shortening and brown sugar into a mixing bowl. Use a spoon or an electric mixer to cream together. Beat in the eggs. Stir in the milk. Add the salt, baking powder, ground cloves, cinnamon and nutmeg. If you really like the taste of these spices, use 1 teaspoon. If you want to tone it down a bit, use 1/2 teaspoon.

Stir in the citron, raisins and chopped walnuts. Stir in the flour until thoroughly combined.

Drop by teaspoonfuls onto a greased baking sheet, and bake at 350 degrees Fahrenheit for 10 or 12 minutes.

Allow to cool thoroughly before storing in an airtight container.

****

Coconut Chocolate Bars

If you need a quick treat, these bars are fairly easy to make. The hardest and longest part of making them is mixing the crust and letting it bake. Be sure to allow the bars to cool before cutting them.

1 cup butter (or 1/2 cup butter and 1/2 cup shortening)
1 cup brown sugar
1 egg
1 teaspoon vanilla
2 cups flour
1/4 teaspoon salt
1 2/3 to 2 cups chocolate chips (milk chocolate or semi-sweet, depending upon your preference; I like milk chocolate because it is sweeter)
2/3 to 1 cup coconut

Thoroughly mix the butter (or butter and shortening), brown sugar, egg and vanilla. Add the flour and salt and mix until a stiff batter is formed. Press the batter into the bottom of a lightly greased 9x13 pan. Bake at 350 degrees Fahrenheit for 25 to 30 minutes.

Turn off the oven. Remove pan and sprinkle chocolate chips over the crust. Return to the oven for 1 or 2 minutes until the chocolate chips have melted. Spread over the crust. Sprinkle coconut over the chocolate. Allow to cool. Cut into bars.

****

Fattigman

Fattigman ("pronounced futty-mun") is a deep-fried Norwegian cookie that my sister made sometimes when I was a kid and that was also served after the Sunday school Christmas program. My mother, who was a first-generation American born to Norwegian immigrants and who spoke only Norwegian at home before she started school, said that fattigman means "poor man's cookies" or "poor man's donuts."

6 egg yolks
1/3 cup sugar
1/2 cup cream
1 tablespoon brandy (or 1 teaspoon brandy extract)
1 teaspoon cardamom (or nutmeg; my mother often substituted nutmeg for cardamom)
1/4 teaspoon salt
2 to 3 cups flour

Beat egg yolks and sugar on high speed with an electric mixer for five minutes. Stir in cream, brandy, and cardamom. Mix in enough flour to make a stiff dough.

Roll dough very thin and cut into two-inch by two-inch pieces. Cut a slit in the middle and pull one of the points through the slit. Deep-fry until golden brown. When cool, sprinkle with powdered sugar. I put powdered sugar in a plastic container with a cover, add some fattigman and shake gently to coat them.

****

Filled Cookies

My dad loved cookies with date filling. My mother or my sister usually only made them at Christmas, and there was no one happier than my father when he had date filled cookies to eat with his coffee on a cold winter's day. In more recent years, I have made filled cookies using homemade jam (blackberry, black raspberry, red raspberry). Below you will also find recipes for plum conserve and for date filling.

3/4 cup butter (softened)
3/4 cup shortening
2 cups sugar
3 eggs
2 teaspoons vanilla
5 cups flour
1 teaspoon baking powder
1/2 teaspoon salt
several tablespoons of milk if the dough seems too dry
Jam: blackberry, black raspberry, strawberry, red raspberry, plum conserve, apple conserve, or date filling (the recipes for plum and apple conserve and date filling are included below)

Heat oven to 350 degrees Fahrenheit. Cream butter, sugar, eggs and vanilla. Stir in flour, baking powder and salt. If the dough is too dry, add 1 or 2 tablespoons of milk. If the dough seems too wet, add 1/4 or 1/2 cup of flour.

Roll out the dough to between 1/8 and 1/4 inch thick. Use either a small round cookie cutter or one large round cutter. Place cookies on an ungreased baking sheet. Put one teaspoon of jam (or other filling) in the middle of the smaller rounds or off to one side of the larger rounds. Place another small round on top of the small rounds; fold the larger rounds in half. Use a fork to crimp the edges together and to poke holes in the top. Bake for 15 minutes, or until light brown.

This recipe makes about six dozen filled cookies. The recipe can also be used to make cut-out Christmas cookies frosted with colored icing.

* *

Plum Conserve

If plum conserve is made specifically for filling cookies, store any that remains in the refrigerator and use on toast or biscuits. The conserve can also be sealed in pint jars. (Makes about three pints.)

8 to 10 fresh, large, ripe plums
1/2 cup of water
4 cups of sugar
2 cups of raisins
1 cup chopped walnuts
2 tablespoons of lemon juice

Pit the plums and chop into small pieces. Place in a large saucepan and add the sugar and water. Boil for 10 minutes, stirring constantly. Add the lemon juice, raisins and walnuts and cook for 10 minutes longer, stirring constantly. (**Note:** Recipe can also be made using 3 cups of chopped apples instead of plums. Add 1/2 teaspoon of cinnamon.)

****

Date Filling

3 cups chopped dates
1/2 cup sugar
1 2/3 cups water
1 tablespoon lemon juice

Put all ingredients into a saucepan and cook over low heat, stirring constantly, until thickened (10 or 15 minutes).

****

Filled Wafer Cookies

These cookies are somewhat labor intensive, but they go well at special events such as a wedding shower or baby shower or a birthday party. For a baby shower, I have divided the cream filling in half and colored one half pink and the other half blue, so that half the cookies have pink filling and half have blue filling. If you are making these for a special event, you may want to consider doubling the recipe.

1 cup soft butter
1/3 cup whipping cream
2 cups flour

Measure the butter, whipping cream and flour into a mixing bowl and stir thoroughly. If the dough seems too soft to roll out, add more flour by 1/4 cup measures until it is the right consistency.

If making a single recipe, roll out about half of the dough at a time. If you are doubling the recipe, roll out 1/4 of the dough.

Roll out on a floured surface to a quarter inch thick or so. Use a very small round cookie cutter to cut out the cookies. I have also used the center round of a doughnut cutter. Place the cookies on an ungreased cookie sheet. Carefully sprinkle a little sugar on the top of each one. Use a fork to prick the top of each cookie so that the top is covered with pricks.

Bake at 350 degrees Fahrenheit for 10 or 12 minutes until the cookies are set but are not browned. Remove from the cookie sheet and allow to cool completely before putting them together with the filling.

Filling
    1/4 cup soft butter
    1 cup powdered sugar
    1 tablespoon milk
    1 teaspoon vanilla

Measure the butter, powdered sugar, milk and vanilla into a mixing bowl. Using an electric mixer, stir on low speed for a minute or so, then beat at high speed until the filling is fluffy. If the filling seems too soft, add more powdered sugar by the tablespoonful until it reaches the desired consistency. Use food coloring to color the filling if desired.

Put the cookies together in pairs with filling in the middle. Store in a covered container.

****

Frying Pan Date Bars

When I was a kid, if Mom had dates on hand to bake with around Christmas time, she had to hide them where Dad wouldn't know to look for them, such as in the dishtowel drawer or behind the pots and pans in the lower cupboard. If she didn't hide the dates, he would open a box and eat them as a snack when he came in for his morning or afternoon coffee break. Not that eating the dates was a bad thing, but if my mother didn't know it, she would be ready to bake something with dates—and would discover that all, or most, of the dates would be gone!

1 beaten egg
1 cup sugar
1/2 cup water
1 1/2 cup chopped dates
1/4 cup butter
4 cups Rice Krispies
1 cup chopped walnuts
1 teaspoon vanilla
1 cup of shredded coconut
more coconut to sprinkle on top

In a small bowl, beat the egg with a fork or an egg beater. Beat in the water. Put the egg and water mixture, sugar, dates and butter into a frying pan. Over medium heat, cook for 4 to 5 minutes, stirring constantly. Add the vanilla. Stir until thoroughly mixed in.

Stir in the Rice Krispies (or similar crispy rice cereal), the walnuts, and the shredded coconut. Spoon into a greased 9x13 pan. Press down with buttered fingers or the back of a spoon. Sprinkle coconut over the top. Allow to chill thoroughly before cutting.

****

Gingersnaps

These cookies are the softer type of Gingersnap, not the hard crispy kind. Soft Gingersnaps were my mother's favorite kind of cookie.

3/4 cup shortening
1 cup brown sugar (packed)
1 egg
1/4 cup molasses
2 1/2 cups flour
2 teaspoons baking soda
1 teaspoon cinnamon
1/2 to 1 teaspoon ginger (depends on how gingery you like your cookies)
1/2 teaspoon cloves
1/4 teaspoon salt
white sugar

Measure the shortening and brown sugar into a mixing bowl and cream together. Stir in the egg and the molasses and mix until thoroughly combined. Add the baking soda, cinnamon, ginger, cloves and salt. Stir in the flour. Mix thoroughly. Dough will be fairly stiff.

Shape dough by rounded teaspoonfuls into balls. Dip the balls into the white sugar and place on a greased cookie sheet, sugar side up. Bake at 350 degrees Fahrenheit for 10 to 12 minutes. Remove from cookie sheet. Allow to cool thoroughly before storing in an airtight container.

✳✳✳✳✳✳✳✳✳✳✳✳✳✳✳✳✳✳✳✳

Lemon Bars

These bars have been a favorite of mine since I was a little kid. (My husband says they are "Randy Recommended").

1 cup butter
1/2 cup powdered sugar
2 cups flour

Use a fork to mix butter into powdered sugar and flour (as if you are mixing pie crust). With your fingers or the back of a spoon, pat into a lightly greased 9x13 inch pan. Bake for 20 minutes at 350 degrees Fahrenheit.

Topping:
  4 eggs
  1/4 cup lemon juice
  2 cups sugar
  1/4 teaspoon salt
  1/4 cup flour
  1 teaspoon baking powder

Measure eggs, lemon juice, sugar, salt, flour and baking powder into a mixing bowl and beat with an electric mixer (or a whisk) until smooth.

Pour over baked crust and bake for 25 minutes at 350 degrees Fahrenheit. Sprinkle powder sugar over the top as soon as you remove the bars from the oven. Allow to cool before cutting.

****

Loretta's Mothball Cookies

From the book *Christmas in Dairyland -- True Stories from a Wisconsin Farm* as mentioned in the story "Good Things Come in Small Packages."

1 cup of butter
1/4 cup of powdered sugar
1 teaspoon vanilla
2 cups flour
1/4 teaspoon salt
2 cups chopped walnuts

Measure the butter and powdered sugar into a mixing bowl. Mix until thoroughly combined. Add the vanilla and stir in. Add the flour, salt and walnuts. Stir in completely. Chill one hour. Form into small balls using about a teaspoon of dough. Place on a greased cookie sheet.

Bake at 250 degrees for 1 hour. Roll in powdered sugar while still warm and again when cool.

****

Loretta's Seven Layer Bars

When I was a kid, my big sister, Loretta, would make these Seven Layer Bars. Of course, a pan didn't last long. Then again, no baked items lasted long around our house.

1/2 cup of butter
1 cup crushed graham crackers
1 six-ounce package of chocolate chips
1 six-ounce package of butterscotch chips
1 cup coconut
1 cup chopped walnuts
1 cup of sweetened, condensed milk

Heat oven to 350 degrees Fahrenheit. Melt the butter in a 9x13 pan in the oven. Remove the pan from the oven and layer other ingredients in the order given. Bake at 350 degrees for 30 minutes.

Allow to cool before cutting.

****

<u>No-Bake Peanut Butter Cookies</u>

Instead of corn flakes cereal, you can also use Wheaties or any other type of flaked cereal.

2 six-ounce packages of butterscotch chips
1 1/2 cups chunky peanut butter
4 to 5 cups of corn flakes
1 cup of dry roasted peanuts

Melt the butterscotch chips and peanut butter together in a saucepan over medium heat or in the microwave. Then stir in 4 to 5 cups of corn flakes and 1 cup of dry roasted peanuts. Drop on wax paper by rounded teaspoonfuls. Allow to cool until set.

Store in an airtight container between layers of wax paper.

✳✳✳✳✳✳✳✳✳✳✳✳✳✳✳✳✳✳✳✳

Oatmeal Peanut Butter Bars
(With fudge frosting)

My husband loves these oatmeal bars and could eat the whole pan by himself. Well. So could I. But I try really hard not to!

1/2 cup butter
1/2 cup shortening
1 cup brown sugar
1 cup white sugar
2 eggs
1 teaspoon vanilla
1/2 cup peanut butter
1 1/2 cups flour
1/2 teaspoon salt
1 teaspoon soda
3 cups dry oatmeal (I have used both quick-cooking and old-fashioned oat meal)

Cream the shortening, butter and sugars. Stir in the eggs, vanilla, and peanut butter. Stir in remaining ingredients. Put in a greased 9x13 pan. Bake at 350 degrees Fahrenheit for 25 to 30 minutes. Let cool. Frost with chocolate frosting.

Note: the batter will puff up as it is baking but as it cools it will fall so that there is a "well" in the pan. Makes the perfect place to pour the chocolate frosting.

Chocolate Frosting:
1 2/3 cup sugar
6 tablespoons butter
6 tablespoons milk
2/3 cup chocolate chips

Boil the sugar, butter and milk for 30 seconds at a full rolling boil that cannot be stirred down. Stir in the chocolate chips until smooth. Pour the frosting over the oatmeal bars and allow to cool before cutting.

****

Oatmeal Jam Bars

When I was growing up, my mother would make homemade strawberry jam and homemade wild blackberry jam and wild pin cherry jelly (when we could find pin cherries). Today, I still pick wild fruit to make jams and jellies. These bars use 1 1/2 to 2 cups of your favorite jam or jelly.

1/2 cup softened butter
1/4 cup shortening
1 cup brown sugar
1 3/4 cups of flour (you can use 1 cup of whole wheat and 3/4 cup of white flour if desired)
1/2 teaspoon salt
1/2 teaspoon baking soda
1 1/2 cups of dry oatmeal (I like to use old-fashioned oatmeal)
1 1/2 cups of your favorite jam or jelly (any flavor; I've used chokecherry jelly, elderberry jelly, grape jelly strawberry jam, raspberry jam, blackberry jam)

Mix the butter, margarine and brown sugar together until smooth. Add the salt, baking soda, flour and oatmeal. Stir until well combined. The mixture will be crumbly. Spread half of the mixture in a greased 9x13 inch pan.

Measure the jam or jelly into a mixing bowl and stir until it is easy to spread. You might need to add a tablespoon of water. Spread the jelly on top of the bottom crust.

Sprinkle the remaining crust on top of the jam/jelly.

Bake at 375 degrees Fahrenheit for 25 to 30 minutes or until the crumble crust is golden brown.

Allow to cool before cutting into bars.

****

Oatmeal Raisin Bars
(With cream cheese frosting)

By now you may have noticed that I have quite a few recipes calling for oatmeal. I learned to eat oatmeal and use it in cooking when I was growing up on our farm. Maybe I have a special affinity for oatmeal, though. My father was harvesting oats on the day I was born.

1 stick butter (softened to room temperature)
1/2 cup shortening
1 cup brown sugar
1/2 cup white sugar
2 eggs
1/4 cup cold water
2 cups flour
1 teaspoon baking soda
1/2 teaspoon salt
1 teaspoon cinnamon
1 teaspoon vanilla
3 cups dry oatmeal (Old-fashioned or quick-cooking)
1 cup raisins

Cream the butter, shortening, brown sugar and white sugar together. Beat in the eggs. Stir in the water. Add the flour, baking soda, salt, cinnamon, vanilla and oatmeal. Stir until thoroughly combined. Stir in the raisins.

Bake at 350 degrees Fahrenheit in a greased 9x13 pan for 25 to 30 minutes or until the bars are set when you tap them with your finger. Allow to cool thoroughly. Frost with cream cheese frosting.

Cream Cheese Frosting:

1 eight-ounce container of soft cream cheese
3 cups powdered sugar
1 tablespoon milk
1/2 teaspoon vanilla

Put cream cheese and 1 cup of the powdered sugar into a mixing bowl. Use an electric mixer and stir until smooth. Add the milk and vanilla. Stir in. Add 2 more cups of powdered sugar. Beat until smooth.

****

Old-Fashioned Sugar Cookies

My grandmother used this recipe for cookies. You can roll them out to make cut-out cookies for Christmas (with frosting and sprinkles!). Or you can roll teaspoonfuls of dough into balls and flatten them with a water glass dipped in sugar. Either way, they are delicious.

1/2 cup of butter (or 1/4 cup butter and 1/4 cup shortening)
1 cup sugar
2 eggs
1 tablespoon of cream (or Half & Half)
2 1/4 cups of flour
1 1/2 teaspoons of baking powder
1/2 teaspoon of nutmeg
1 1/2 teaspoons of lemon extract (if you want a less lemony taste, use lemon juice)

Cream together shortening (butter or margarine), sugar, eggs and cream. Mix in the dry ingredients and the lemon extract or the lemon juice. Work the dough with your hands for a minute before rolling out the cookies.

Bake on greased baking sheet at Fahrenheit degrees for 10 minutes.

A single recipe makes about three dozen cookies.

****

Old-Fashioned Oatmeal Cookies

These cookies were another specialty my sister made when I was growing up.

1/2 cup butter
1/2 cup shortening
1 cup brown sugar
1/2 cup white sugar
1 egg
1 teaspoon salt
3/4 teaspoon cinnamon
1/4 teaspoon ground cloves
1/2 teaspoon baking soda
1 teaspoon vanilla
1 cup raisins (optional)
1 cup chopped walnuts (optional)
1 cup flour
3 cups dry oatmeal (either quick-cooking or old fashioned; I like to use old-fashioned)

Measure the butter, shortening, brown sugar and white sugar into a mixing bowl. Cream together. Beat in the egg. Add the salt, cinnamon, cloves, baking soda and vanilla. Stir in the flour, raisins and walnuts. Stir in the oatmeal until thoroughly combined.

Drop by teaspoonfuls onto a greased cookie sheet and bake at 350 degrees Fahrenheit for about 10 minutes or until "set" when tapped with your finger. Immediately remove the baking sheet and allow to cool before storing.

****

Peanut Butter Bars

Peanut butter bars with peanut butter frosting. Yum! Peanut butter was another thing I learned to love while growing up on our farm. My dad really liked peanut butter, too.

1 cup brown sugar
1/2 cup shortening
1 cup peanut butter
1 egg
1 teaspoon vanilla
1 1/2 cups flour
1 teaspoon baking soda
1/4 teaspoon salt
1/2 cup oatmeal

Measure the brown sugar, shortening and peanut butter into a mixing bowl and cream together. Beat in the egg. Add the vanilla, flour, baking soda, salt and oatmeal. Stir until thoroughly combined.

Spoon into a greased 9x13 pan. Bake at 350 degrees Fahrenheit for 20 to 25 minutes.

Cool before frosting.

Frosting:
2 tablespoons soft butter
1/2 cup peanut butter
2 cups powdered sugar
3 tablespoons milk

Cream the butter and peanut butter together. Add the powdered sugar and milk. Beat on high speed with an electric mixer for a minute or two. If the frosting seems too thin, add more powdered sugar by tablespoons. If the frosting seems too thick, add more milk by tablespoons. Beat until the frosting reaches the desired consistency.

****

Peanut Butter Cookies

My idea of "comfort food!" My big sister, Loretta used to bake lots of peanut butter cookies, too, when I was a kid. I was always fascinated with the criss-cross pattern made with a fork.

1/2 cup butter
1/2 cup shortening
1 cup peanut butter
1 cup white sugar
1 cup brown sugar
2 eggs
3 to 3 1/2 cups of flour (if the cookie dough seems too soft, add another 1/2 cup of flour)
1/2 teaspoon baking soda
1/2 teaspoon baking powder
1/4 teaspoon salt

Mix the butter, shortening, peanut butter and white and brown sugars together until thoroughly creamed. Beat in the eggs. Add the flour, baking soda, baking powder and salt.

Shape small teaspoonfuls of dough into balls. Place on a lightly greased cookie sheet. With a fork dipped in flour, flatten the cookies in crisscross patterns. Bake 10 to 12 minutes at 350 degrees Fahrenheit.

Makes 4 to 6 dozen cookies, depending on how big you like your peanut butter cookies.

****

Peanut Butter Macaroons
(No-Bake Cookies)

These cookies are chewy-delicious. A good source of calcium, too!

1 cup peanut butter
1 cup corn syrup
1 1/2 cups powdered milk
1/4 cup milk
4 to 5 cups Rice Krispies or Special-K cereal (as a substitute for the Rice Krispies, I have used 2 cups of Grapenuts or generic Grapenuts-type cereal)
shredded coconut to roll the cookies in

Measure the peanut butter, corn syrup, powdered milk and milk into a medium-sized mixing bowl and mix thoroughly (mixture will be stiff and sticky). Add the cereal. Stir until well combined.
Shape the cookies into balls about half the size of an egg. Roll in shredded coconut. Place on a cookie sheet and allow to set for several hours. Store in a loosely covered container.

****

Sandbakelse
(The Easy Way!)

Pronounced "sun-buckles"— traditionally, these Norwegian almond flavored cookies are made in little fluted tins. My mother would never make sandbakelse because she said they were too much work. More recently, a friend of mine, who also is of Norwegian heritage, says she only makes a few tins for Christmas "just because" and then rolls the rest of the dough into balls and bakes them that way. What a great idea! They are delicious!

> **3/4 cup butter**
> **3/4 cup sugar**
> **1 egg**
> **1/4 teaspoon salt**
> **1/2 teaspoon almond extract**
> **1/2 cup of slivered almonds chopped fine**
> **2 cups flour**

Measure the butter and sugar into a mixing bowl and cream together. Beat in the egg and the almond extract. Add the flour, salt and chopped almonds. Stir until thoroughly combined.

Roll dough into balls by small teaspoonfuls and bake on an ungreased cookie sheet at 350 degrees Fahrenheit for 12 or 13 minutes or until cookies are fairly crisp.

To make traditional sandbakelse:
Pack dough into sandbakelse molds about 1/8 inch thick on the bottom and sides of mold. Place on a cookie sheet and bake at 350 degrees Fahrenheit for 12 or 15 minutes until the cookies are crispy. Allow to cool. Carefully tap the molds to loosen the cookies. Good luck.

****

Scotch Shortbread

A not-too-sweet and very easy-to-roll rolled cookie. Use Christmas cookie cutters for Christmas or heart-shaped cutters for Valentine's Day or an ordinary round cookie or biscuit cutter for cookies any time.

1/2 cup butter
1/3 cup sugar
3/4 cup shortening
3 cups flour
3/4 cup milk

Cream the butter, shortening and sugar. Mix in the flour. Stir in the milk.

Flour the surface where you will roll the cookies. Roll out the dough to about 1/3 inch thick. Cut out cookies in various shapes. Bake on an ungreased cookie sheet at 350 degrees Fahrenheit for 20 minutes. Immediately remove from the cookie sheet and allow to cool. Frost with powdered sugar icing.

Makes about 4 dozen cookies.

Frosting:
3 tablespoons soft butter
2 cups powdered sugar
3 tablespoons milk
Food coloring (if desired)

Cream the butter into the powdered sugar. Add milk. Beat on high speed with an electric mixer for a minute or two. If the frosting seems too thin, add more powdered sugar by tablespoons. If the frosting seems too thick, add more milk by tablespoons. Beat until the frosting reaches the desired consistency. Stir in food coloring if you want.

Lemon icing: When the frosting is mixed, add a few drops of lemon extract or 1 to 2 teaspoons of lemon juice and stir until thoroughly combined. Yellow food coloring works nicely to color lemon icing.

****

Shamrock Cookie Recipe

You can use your heart-shaped cookie cutter to make Shamrock Cookies for St. Patrick's Day. The cookies turn out to be quite large—just the right size for beating the winter blues in March when you can hardly wait for spring to arrive!

1/2 cup shortening
1/2 cup butter
2 cups sugar
3 eggs
1/4 cup milk
1 teaspoon vanilla
1/2 teaspoon salt
5 cups flour

Cream shortening and sugar together. Beat in eggs. Stir in milk, vanilla and salt. Mix in flour. Work the dough with your hands for a minute before rolling out. Roll out the dough to 1/8 inch thick. Use flour as needed to roll out the cookies.

For each shamrock, you will need 3 heart-shaped cookies. Place one heart on an ungreased cookie sheet, then put one heart on each side at a 90-degree angle so the tips at the bottom are overlapping. Gently press the cookies together where they overlap. Roll a lump of dough the size of a small walnut into a rope. Press one inch of the rope onto the bottom of the shamrock. Shape the remaining rope into a stem and flatten gently. (Four or five shamrocks will fit on a cookie sheet.)

Bake in a 350 degree Fahrenheit oven for 12 minutes, or until golden brown. Immediately remove the cookies from the cookie sheet and allow to cool. When the cookies are cooled thoroughly, frost with shamrock icing. For added decoration, use cookie sprinkles, if desired.

Shamrock Icing
(makes enough to frost 2 dozen shamrock cookies)
3 cups of powdered sugar
1/4 cup soft butter or margarine
5 or 6 tablespoons milk
1/4 teaspoon salt
1/2 teaspoon vanilla
10 drops green food coloring

Measure the powdered sugar into a mixing bowl. Work the butter/margarine into the dry powdered sugar with a mixing spoon. Add salt and vanilla. Add the milk 1 tablespoon at a time and mix thoroughly after each addition. If the icing seems too thin, add more powdered sugar by the tablespoon. If it seems too thick, add more milk by the tablespoon. When the icing reaches the desired consistency, add the food coloring and mix thoroughly.

****

Snickerdoodles

My sister used to make Snickerdoodles when I was a kid, and I always thought it was such a funny name! Good cookies, though. Instead of half butter and half shortening, you can use all butter if want.

1/2 cup of butter (softened)
1/2 cup shortening
1 1/2 cups sugar
2 eggs
2 1/2 cups flour
2 teaspoons cream of tartar
1 teaspoon baking soda
1/4 teaspoon salt
2 tablespoons sugar
2 teaspoons ground cinnamon

Measure the butter and shortening into a mixing bowl. Cream together. Add the sugar. Cream together. Beat in the eggs. Stir in the flour, cream of tartar, baking soda and salt.

Mix sugar and cinnamon in a small bowl.

Shape dough by rounded teaspoonfuls into balls and roll in sugar and cinnamon. Bake on an ungreased baking sheet at 350 degrees Fahrenheit for 10 to 12 minutes or until set and light golden brown.

Remove from cookie sheet immediately. Allow to cool thoroughly. Store in an airtight container.

****

Chocolate Waffle (Iron) Cookies

I loved to make these when I was a kid. There was just something about baking cookies on a waffle iron that made it seem like so much fun. Frost with vanilla or chocolate frosting if desired.

1 cup brown sugar
1/2 cup Canola oil (or another vegetable oil)
1 1/2 cups flour
2 eggs
1 teaspoon baking powder
3 to 4 tablespoons cocoa (depending on how much chocolate you want in your cookies)
1 teaspoon vanilla
1/2 cup milk
1/4 teaspoon salt

Measure brown sugar and oil into a mixing bowl. Cream together. Beat in eggs. Add baking powder, vanilla, cocoa and salt. Add the milk and flour. Mix until thoroughly combined. Heat the waffle iron.

Drop by teaspoonfuls onto the hot waffle iron. The waffle iron we had when I was a kid was a big, square iron that made double waffles. The one I have now is smaller and round with four pie-shaped "wedges," so I bake four cookies at a time.

Bake the same as you would waffles. When the waffle iron "clicks" off, check the cookies. If you want a cookie that's crispier, leave them in the waffle iron for another minute or so. Gently remove the cookies with a fork. Set waffle cookies aside and allow to cool. Frost with white frosting or chocolate frosting or dust with powdered sugar.

Frosting:
2 tablespoons soft butter
2 cups powdered sugar
2 tablespoons milk
1 teaspoon vanilla
dash of salt
(for chocolate frosting, add 1 tablespoon cocoa)

Measure all ingredients into a mixing bowl and whip with an electric mixer for 1 to 2 minutes.

****

Walnut Bars

These bars are a little like "pecan pie in a pan." Maybe that's because whenever I make pecan pie, I usually use walnuts instead of pecans! At any rate, these bars are delicious.

1/2 cup butter
1 cup shortening
1 1/2 cups powdered sugar
3 cups flour
3 eggs
1 1/2 cups brown sugar
3 tablespoons flour
1/2 teaspoon baking powder
1/2 teaspoon salt
1 teaspoon vanilla
1 1/2 cups chopped walnuts

Cream butter and shortening together. Mix in powdered sugar. Use a fork to work in the flour. Mixture will be crumbly. Press into an ungreased 9x13 inch pan. Bake at 325 degrees for 25 to 30 minutes.

When the crust is half finished baking, break the eggs into a clean mixing bowl. Beat the eggs with an electric mixer for a couple of minutes. Stir in the brown sugar, flour, baking powder, salt vanilla and chopped walnuts. Spread over the hot crust as soon as you take it out of the oven. Bake an additional 20 to 25 minutes or until set.

Allow to cool before cutting.

****

Whole Wheat Butterscotch Bars

This recipe is baked in an 8-inch by 8-inch pan. To make a 9x13 inch pan of bars, double the recipe.

1/4 cup canola oil (or other cooking oil)
1 cup brown sugar
1 egg
3/4 cup whole wheat flour
1 teaspoon vanilla
1/2 teaspoon baking powder
1/4 teaspoon salt
1 cup chopped walnuts

Measure all ingredients into a mixing bowl, except for the walnuts. Stir until thoroughly combined. Stir in the walnuts.

Spread in a greased 8x8 inch pan.

Bake at 350 degrees Fahrenheit for 25 minutes.

****

Jams, Jellies, Pickles & Miscellaneous

Apple Butter

You can use commercially prepared applesauce for this recipe, or if you like, you can make your own applesauce. Since the "Apple Butter" recipe calls for 10 cups of sugar, if you are making your own applesauce, you might want to consider not putting any sugar into the sauce.

Applesauce: When I make applesauce, I do not peel the apples. I wash them off, cut them in half and in quarters, remove the seeds and core, and cut the apple slices into small pieces. Then I add a quarter cup of cold water for every four or five apples and let them simmer over medium heat, stirring them every once in a while, until the apples have cooked down into applesauce (15 to 20 minutes or so, depending on the variety of the apple). If I'm making sweetened applesauce, I add a quarter to a third of a cup of brown sugar for every four or five apples.

12 cups of applesauce
10 cups sugar
1/2 cup vinegar
1/2 to 1 teaspoon cinnamon (if you like lots of cinnamon flavor, use 1 teaspoon)
1/4 to 1/2 teaspoon ground cloves
1/4 teaspoon salt

Combine all ingredients in a large kettle and cook for 20 to 25 minutes over medium heat, stirring as needed to keep it from burning to the bottom of the pan.

Fill clean jars. Seal with new lids and rings. Process in a boiling water bath for 10 minutes.

Recipe makes approximately 10 pints of apple butter.

****

How To Make Candles Using Old Crayons

From the book *Christmas in Dairyland (True Stories from a Wisconsin Farm)*
(copyright 2003; LeAnn R. Ralph)

We made these candles when I was a kid, and since then, I've made them a couple more times. I'm happy to say that they are still as much fun to make as they always were!

   1 wax carton (quart) (milk, fabric softener, or orange juice)
   1 pound of paraffin wax
   4 or 5 old crayons
   two trays of ice cubes
   a double boiler (or an empty coffee can and a saucepan)
   1 piece of ordinary white package string about six inches long

Caution: Do not heat paraffin directly over the burner. Paraffin is easily combustible. Use a double boiler or a two-pound coffee can set in a pan of water. I put the coffee can on top of home canning jar rings. If the can is not set on top of something, the concave bottom creates a vacuum when the water begins to heat, plus if it's on the bottom of the pan, it's just that much closer to the burner.

Trim off the top of the carton so that it is about six inches high. Cut the string so that it is six inches long. (To make a wick that lasts longer, try braiding three pieces of string together.)

Melt the paraffin wax over medium heat in a double boiler or a coffee can in a pan of water. Use three-quarters of a pound for a somewhat smaller candle or use all four squares for a larger candle. Once the water begins to boil, it will take 10 or 15 minutes for the paraffin to melt.

Break the crayons into small pieces and add to the paraffin. If the crayons are added first before the wax is melted, the color makes it difficult to see if all of the paraffin is liquefied. Use a pair of tongs (a scissors works, too), and dip the string into the paraffin. Dipping the string will ensure that it is coated with paraffin since the ice cubes may prevent some sections from coming in contact with the liquid wax. Hold the string so that it is in the middle of the carton and fill the carton with ice cubes. Pour the hot paraffin over the ice cubes.

The candle will be set in about 30 minutes. Let the candle stand for another hour or two until most of the ice cubes are melted. Pour off the water. Peel off the carton. Place the candle in a tray or on a plate to catch the rest of the water from the ice cubes. Let the candle dry for a day or two.

The candles I have made with a single piece of string only burn for an hour or so and burn quickly enough so that most of the paraffin remains intact. To use the paraffin again, melt the candle and pour the wax into other glass or metal containers to make solid candles. Tie the wick to a pencil and place the pencil across the top of the glass or metal container. Or melt the used ice candle and make another one.

****

Homemade Dill Pickles

I have always loved dill pickles! It would seem that other people do, too. Whenever we have a church dinner, we serve dill pickles, and they usually don't last long.

Brine:
   1/2 cup pickling salt (don't use iodized salt; your pickles will get mushy)
   3 cups vinegar
   13 cups water
   1/2 cup sugar

Combine and heat through.

To pack each jar:

   1/2 teaspoon of powdered alum
   2 to 4 onion slices
   1 or 2 heads of dill (or 1 teaspoon of dill seed)
   1 peeled whole clove of garlic
   small to medium size scrubbed cucumbers to fill the jar

Pack each jar with the above ingredients in the order given. Pour enough hot brine into each jar to fill the jar. Seal with lids and rings. Place in a boiling water bath for 10 minutes.

One brine recipe makes enough for 7 or 8 quarts, depending on how tightly you pack the jars.

Let the jars sit for a week or two before eating the pickles. The pickled onion slices are good to eat, too, and are especially good on sandwiches.

****

Pickled Beets

Pickled beets were one of my dad's favorite kind of pickles. He raised the beets in our garden, and then my mother would can pickled beets. You can also use this brine for green beans, wax beans and carrots.

2 cups water
2 cups vinegar
2 cups sugar
1 teaspoon salt
whole cloves
cinnamon

For pickled beets: scrub the beets and boil until tender with the peeling on. <u>Do not</u> cut off the stem end or the root end. When cool, peel the beets. Cut into slices.

Combine the above ingredients in a kettle and heat until boiling.

Add several whole cloves and 1/4 teaspoon cinnamon to the jar. Pack the jar with beet slices. Pour hot syrup over the beets. Seal with lids and rings. Place in a boiling water bath for 10 minutes.

This recipe makes enough brine for approximately 6 pints of pickled beets or 3 quarts of pickled beets.

For green beans, wax beans or carrots: cook the vegetables in boiling water for a couple of minutes. You do not want to cook them so long that the vegetables are soft and mushy, just until they are about half cooked. Then pack the jars as you would for beets and process in a boiling water bath for 10 minutes.

✳✳✳✳✳✳✳✳✳✳✳✳✳✳✳✳✳✳✳

Refrigerator Pickles

This is a quick and easy way to make pickled cucumber slices without packing them in jars and sealing the jars.

6 cups of cucumber slices
2 medium onions sliced thin
2 green peppers cut into thin slices (optional)
canning salt (or Kosher salt) (regular table salt will make your refrigerator pickles mushy)

Place all ingredients in a large bowl in layers. Sprinkle layers with salt. Cover with ice water. Let stand for 2 hours and drain.

Brine:
2 cups sugar
1 cup vinegar
1 teaspoon celery seed

Measure into a mixing bowl and stir until sugar is dissolved. Pour over cucumbers. Store in the refrigerator in a covered container.

Note: The cucumbers do not have to be peeled. The peeling adds another source of fiber to your diet. Also, be sure to cut off enough of the ends to remove the bitter part of the cucumber.

****

Rhubarb Marmalade

If you like regular orange marmalade, you might want to try this recipe for rhubarb marmalade. It's good on toast, but I like it on waffles and pancakes, too. This recipe makes about 3 pints of rhubarb marmalade. I have Canadian red rhubarb. If you have other varieties with more of a green stalk, add a few drops of red food coloring to the recipe.

4 cups of rhubarb (cut up in small pieces)
4 cups sugar
3 medium to large oranges
1 cup of water
2 tablespoons of cornstarch (optional at the end)

Wash the rhubarb and cut up into small pieces. Wash the oranges and cut up into small pieces, rind and all. (If there are seeds, remove the seeds.)

Combine all ingredients (except the cornstarch) in a large saucepan or a small kettle. Bring to a boil and cook over medium heat for 45 minutes. Stir occasionally at the beginning and stir more frequently toward the end of the cooking period. If the marmalade starts to stick, turn the burner down to medium low or low heat.

If a thicker marmalade is desired, mix the cornstarch into 1/4 cup of cold water. While stirring the marmalade, slowly pour the cornstarch mixture into the marmalade and continue cooking for a few minutes until thicker.

Instead of adding cornstarch, you can also cook the marmalade for another 15 to 30 minutes to reach the desired consistency.

Seal in sterilized jars. Process the jars in a boiling water bath for 10 minutes. Makes about 3 pints.

Instead of a boiling water bath, after I have put the lids on the jars, I sometimes put the jars into a cake pan with a couple of inches or water and put them in the oven at 350 degrees Fahrenheit for 10 to 15 minutes.

****

Sweet Glazed Pickles

These pickles are somewhat time-consuming, but they are delicious! When I say "time-consuming"—from start to finish takes 12 days. But the pickles are very pretty in the jar when you use green food coloring—a dark, almost forest green.

Step 1:
Select as many cucumbers as you want to make pickles. One gallon (four quarts) of cucumbers will make three to four quarts of pickles (or six to eight pints).

Scrub the cucumbers in cold water with a brush. Soak the cucumbers in a brine of 1 cup of pickling salt (don't use iodized salt, your pickles will be soft) to 9 cups of water <u>for three days</u>. Make enough brine to cover all of the cucumbers.

Step 2:
On the fourth day, drain the cucumbers and cover with fresh water <u>for three days</u>. Change the water every day.

Step 3:
On the seventh day, cut the cucumbers into chunks. For each quart of cucumber chunks, allow 1 teaspoon of alum, 1 quart of vinegar and 2 quarts of water. Put cucumber chunks in the alum, vinegar and water mixture and let stand <u>for 2 days</u>. Drain.

Step 4:
Make a syrup of 3 cups of sugar, 2 cups of vinegar and 1 tablespoon of mixed pickling spices. Let this boil for 1 minute. Double, triple or quadruple the recipe (or whatever) so you have enough to cover the cucumbers. Put the cucumbers in the syrup and heat until almost to the point of boiling.

Step 5:
For the next <u>two days</u>, drain the syrup off the pickles, reheat, and pour over the pickles again.

Step 6:
On the third day, the pickles may be reheated and canned. For deep green pickles, add green food coloring as desired when you are reheating them before canning.

****

Tomato Preserves

If you like tomatoes, here's a different way to serve them. I like to eat tomato preserves on toast, biscuits, pancakes and waffles. We always used to have lots of tomatoes—the big red slicers—from the garden on our farm. Nowadays I raise Roma tomatoes.

6 cups tomatoes (chopped or processed in the blender)
4 cups sugar
2 3-ounce package of lemon-flavored gelatin
1/4 cup of lemon juice

Put tomatoes and sugar into a kettle and boil for 12 minutes, stirring constantly. Add gelatin and lemon juice. Stir until the gelatin is dissolved.

Seal in jars. Process in a boiling water bath for 10 minutes.

Note: When you are ready to eat a jar of tomato preserves, put the jar in the refrigerator for four hours first. The preserves will firm up in the refrigerator. Keep the jar refrigerated after opening it.

Note: one recipe makes 4 to 5 pints of tomato preserves. Also, you do not have to peel the tomatoes. Leaving the peeling on adds more fiber to the tomato preserves.

****

Norwegian Foods

Christmas Bread

This recipe makes two large loaves. When I was a kid, my mother, who was the daughter of Norwegian immigrants, would bake Christmas Bread starting around December 1. Instead of regular bread, much of the bread she would bake in December would be Christmas Bread. It is good toasted but also good just plain with butter.

2 cups warm water
2 packages of dry yeast
1/4 cup sugar
1 teaspoon salt
2 eggs
1/2 cup shortening (I have also used Canola oil)
1 to 2 cups of citron (the mixture you can buy nowadays is not pure citron, but is generally known as "fruit cake mix" and contains other ingredients besides citron) (if you really like the taste, add 2 cups)
6 to 7 cups of flour

Dissolve the yeast in warm water in a large mixing bowl. Add 2 cups of flour, sugar, eggs, salt, shortening/oil and beat until smooth. Either use an electric mixer or beat by hand. Add the citron. Add 4 cups of flour. If you're using an electric mixer, you will need the dough hooks by this point. Mix thoroughly

Turn dough out onto a floured surface. Knead for 10 minutes. If dough becomes too sticky, knead in an-other 1/2 to 1 cup of flour. Put in a greased bowl and cover with a towel. Let rise in a warm place for 45 minutes to an hour.

Punch down dough. Knead for a minute or two. Shape into loaves. If you want larger loaves, divide dough in half and make two loaves. For smaller loaves, divide the dough into three equal pieces or four equal pieces.

Place dough in greased loaf pans and let rise for 45 minutes. Bake at 350 degrees Fahrenheit for 35 to 45 minutes or until the loaves turn brown and sound hollow when tapped with your forefinger. Turn bread out of the pans. Brush with shortening to help keep the crust soft. Allow the bread to cool before slicing it.

✳✳✳✳✳✳✳✳✳✳✳✳✳✳✳✳✳✳✳✳

Fattigman

Fattigman (pronounced "futty-mun") is a deep-fried Norwegian cookie that my sister made sometimes when I was a kid and that was also served after the Sunday school Christmas program. Loretta made them because Mom said they were too much work, although it didn't seem to me that they were more work than lefse, and Mom made lefse. I think maybe she just didn't like to make them. Mom said Fattigman means "poor man's cookies" or "poor man's donuts." Since Fattigman contain egg yolks and cream and are deep-fat fried, they can by no stretch of the imagination be considered "good for you" — although I have to say there isn't much that I make at Christmastime that can be considered healthy. Except for Sweet Soup, I suppose.

**6 egg yolks
1/3 cup sugar
1/2 cup cream
1 tablespoon brandy (or 1 teaspoon brandy extract)
1 teaspoon cardamom (or nutmeg; my mother often substituted nutmeg in recipes that called for cardamom)
1/4 teaspoon salt
2 to 3 cups flour**

Beat the egg yolks and sugar on high speed with an electric mixer for five minutes. Stir in cream, brandy, and cardamom. Mix in enough flour to make a stiff dough.

Roll the dough out very thin on a floured surface and cut into two-inch by two-inch pieces. Cut a slit in the middle and pull one of the points through the slit. Deep-fry until crispy and golden brown. When cool, sprinkle with powdered sugar. (I put powdered sugar in a plastic container with a cover, add some fattigman and shake gently to coat them.)

Store in a covered container.

****

Julekake

The difference between julekake and Norwegian Christmas bread is that julekake is a richer bread, almost more like a pastry or a dessert rather than bread. This recipe makes two large round loaves. If you want, divide the dough into four smaller loaves.

2 cups milk
1 cup sugar
1/2 cup butter
2 packages of yeast
1/2 cup warm water
1 teaspoon salt
1 teaspoon cardamom (substitute cinnamon and/or nutmeg if you prefer)
7 cups flour
1 cup of raisins
1/2 cup of citron (fruit cake mix)
1/2 cup of red candied cherries
1/2 cup of green candied cherries

In a medium saucepan, heat the butter, milk, sugar and salt until the butter has melted. Pour the milk mixture into a large bowl and let it cool.

Dissolve the yeast in the warm water and add it to the milk mixture. Add the cardamom (or other spices) and 3 cups of flour and beat until smooth. Mix in the fruit and 4 cups of flour. Knead the dough for about 10 minutes. If the dough becomes too sticky, knead in another 1/4 to 1/2 cup of flour.

Put the dough in a greased bowl and cover and let it rise in a warm place until doubled, or about one hour.

Punch down the dough and divide in half. Knead for a minute or two, and then form each half into rounds—or into four loaves, if you prefer. Place the dough on a large greased cookie sheet and let rise for 45 minutes. (The loaves will become very large, so be careful not to put them too close to the edge of the cookie sheet.)

Bake at 350 degrees Fahrenheit for 40 to 45 minutes. If the loaves start turning too brown, turn the oven down to 325. After you remove the loaves from the oven, brush them with shortening while they are still hot. This will help the crust to stay soft. Remove loaves from the cookie sheet. Allow the julekake to cool before slicing.

If you prefer, after the julekake is cool, drizzle on powdered sugar icing and decorate with cherries, walnuts or pecans. (**Icing:** 2 cups powdered sugar; 1 teaspoon vanilla; add water or milk by the teaspoon and stir thoroughly. Keep adding water or milk until the icing reaches the right consistency to drizzle over the Julekake.

* *

Lefse

This recipe is from my book *Christmas In Dairyland*. Chapter 1 is called "The Lefse Connection."

When I was a kid growing up on our small dairy farm in Wisconsin that had been homesteaded by Norwegian immigrants in the late 1800s, I figured everyone knew how to make lefse. After all, everyone I knew could make lefse, so didn't that mean everyone else could make it too?

That was forty years ago.

Now I know better.

In the rural area where I live, however, at least a few people still do know how to make lefse. And at Christmas, you can even buy lefse in some of the grocery stores around here. Lefse is a flat potato pastry. I have also heard lefse described as "Norwegian tortillas."

Expert lefse makers use a lefse griddle (a large, round electric griddle that heats up to 500 degrees), a grooved lefse rolling pin, and flat wooden lefse turners. But you don't have to buy special equipment to make lefse. You can use ordinary kitchen utensils: an electric fry pan (that heats up to 400 or 450 degrees Fahrenheit), a rolling pin, a pancake turner, and a large mixing bowl. You will also need potatoes, butter or margarine, a little sugar, some milk, and flour.

Rolling lefse is a skill that requires plenty of patience and lots of practice. Expert lefse makers produce pieces that are as large as the top of a snare drum and practically thin enough to read a newspaper through. My lefse, which turns out just like my mother's did, is about the size of a dinner plate and somewhat thicker.

Lefse experts recommend ricing the cooked potatoes, but my mother always mashed the potatoes. Refrigerating the mashed or riced potatoes overnight makes the lefse easier to roll out.

When you're ready to start making lefse, take the potatoes out of the refrigerator and mash or rice them again. I have one of those crisscross patterned potato mashers, and it works well for taking the lumps out of the mashed potatoes. Lefse rolls out easier if the dough is cold, so make sure the potatoes are cold when you start. You may also want to refrigerate the dough for a while after you mix it. I have noticed that when I reach the end of the batch and the dough is starting to warm up, the lefse is harder to roll out.

Making a batch of lefse from this recipe takes about one and a half hours and will yield approximately two dozen pieces, depending upon how much dough you use for each one.

Here is my mother's recipe for lefse:

4 heaping cups of mashed or riced potatoes
1 stick of butter
1/3 cup of milk
1 teaspoon of sugar
1 teaspoon of salt
2 cups of flour
extra flour for rolling out the dough

Measure out the mashed/riced potatoes into a large mixing bowl. In a medium-sized saucepan, melt the butter in the milk; stir in the sugar and salt. Then pour over the cold mashed (riced) potatoes and mix.

Stir two cups of flour into the potato mixture. The dough will be sticky and soft.

Start heating the griddle or electric frying pan. Do not add any oil, margarine or shortening. Lefse is baked on a dry surface.

Take a lump of dough about the size of an egg. Place a heaping teaspoon of flour on the surface where you're going to roll out your lefse. Work about half of the heaping teaspoon of flour into the lump of dough (enough so you can handle the dough, but not so much that the dough becomes dry).

Starting in the center, roll outward until the lefse is about the size of a dinner plate. Try not to roll the lefse so thin that you cannot pick it up. If the lefse tears when you start to pick it up, gather it into a lump and roll it out again. Don't do this too many times, though, or your lefse will end up tough and dry. Ideally, you should only roll the lefse once, although that's probably not a realistic expectation if you've never made lefse before. Also try to turn the lefse only once while you are rolling it out. If the lefse starts to stick, add a little more flour.

When you have the lefse rolled out, transfer it to the hot griddle. Carefully pick it up and quickly move it. If you move slowly, the lefse is more likely to tear. Expert lefse makers use flat lefse turners (they look like long flat sticks) to transfer the dough by rolling it onto the turner and then unrolling it onto the griddle. You can also try rolling your lefse onto the rolling pin and transferring it to the griddle or the fry pan.

Once you have the lefse on the griddle, bake it for about a minute, just until brown 'freckles' start to appear; then turn the lefse over and let the other side bake just until brown freckles start to appear. While the first piece of lefse is baking, roll out your second one.

After the first piece of lefse is done, use the pancake turner to remove it from the griddle and place it on a clean dishtowel. Cover with another dishtowel.

Bake the second lefse and roll out the third piece.

When the second lefse is finished, place it on top of the first one and cover with the towel again. Then bake the third piece.

Repeat until you have baked all of the dough. Place each newly baked lefse on top of the previously baked lefse and cover the stack with the towel.

Once the lefse is completely cool, place it in a plastic bag or wrap it with plastic wrap or aluminum foil to help keep it moist. You must wait until the lefse is completely cool before wrapping it, otherwise the heat from the lefse will condense inside of the plastic or the aluminum foil, and your lefse will end up soggy. If you leave the lefse overnight without wrapping it in plastic or aluminum foil, it will probably be dried out in the morning. If the lefse dries out, sprinkle a little water on the dishtowel and wrap the dishtowel and the lefse in plastic. The lefse will soften up again.

When you're ready to eat a piece of lefse, spread it with butter, sprinkle sugar on it (some people also like to sprinkle cinnamon on their lefse), and roll into a log.

Also, once the lefse is cool, it can be frozen.

****

Norwegian Christmas Cookies

My mother liked to use fruit cake mix, which has chopped red and green citron in it, for her Christmas baking. These cookies can be made into wreaths or made into round cookies.

1 cup butter (softened)
1/2 cup shortening
1 cup sugar
2 eggs
2 teaspoons grated orange peel (if desired)
1 teaspoon baking powder
1/2 teaspoon cardamom (or use cinnamon or nutmeg, if your prefer)
1 teaspoon vanilla
1 cup fruit cake mix (or use chopped red and green candied cherries)
1 cup chopped walnuts
4 cups flour

Cream the shortening, butter and sugar together. Beat in the eggs. Stir in the orange peel (if desired), baking powder, cardamom (cinnamon or nutmeg) and vanilla. Add the fruit cake mix (or candied cherries) and the walnuts. Whether you use fruit cake mix or candied cherries, be sure it is chopped into small pieces. Stir in the flour.

Wreaths: roll one teaspoonful of dough into a six-inch rope. Shape into a circle, cross the ends and press together where the ends meet, leaving a small amount of dough extending down from either side of where dough is pressed together. Sprinkle with red or green sugar and/or decorate with cinnamon candies or other cookie sprinkles if desired.

Round cookies: shape teaspoons of dough into small balls. Press with the bottoms of a drinking glass dipped into sugar.

Bake at 350 degrees Fahrenheit on an ungreased baking sheet for 10 to 12 minutes (or until lightly browned on the bottom). Remove from the cookie sheet immediately and allow to cool. Store in a covered container. These cookies freeze well.

* * * * * * * * * * * * * * * * * * * *

Norwegian Cucumber Salad

When I was a kid growing up on our farm, Dad always raised cucumbers in the garden. My mother canned some of them as dill pickles. This recipe is how we often ate fresh cucumbers from the garden for dinner or supper.

1/2 cup water
1/2 cup vinegar
1/2 cup white sugar
1/4 to 1/2 teaspoon salt
1/4 teaspoon ground black pepper
3 to 4 large cucumbers

Measure the water, vinegar, sugar, salt and pepper into a saucepan and bring to a boil.

Scrub the cucumbers. Cut off the bitter ends of the cucumbers. Do not peel the cucumbers. Cut into thin slices. Put the slices into a bowl and pour the hot liquid over the cucumbers. Allow to cool and then chill in the refrigerator. Serve when completely chilled.

****

Norwegian Flat Bread

Flat Bread was a staple among many of the old Norwegian families in this area. Sometimes it was called "hard tack." Serve pieces of Flat Bread spread with butter and sprinkled with sugar, and cinnamon, if desired. The old-timers used lard in their flat bread recipes.

1 1/2 cups cornmeal
3 cups flour
2 tablespoons sugar
1 teaspoon salt
1/2 cup shortening
1 1/2 cups boiling water

In a mixing bowl, stir together cornmeal, flour, sugar and salt.

Make a hole in the middle of the mixture and place 1/2 cup of shortening in the hole. Pour 1 1/2 cups of boiling water over the shortening. Let stand for a few minutes until the shortening melts. Stir together thoroughly. Use your hands to knead the dough for a minute or two if this seems easier than stirring the dough.

Divide the dough into pieces the size of a large egg. Roll out into thin pieces on a floured surface and bake on a lefse griddle, in a cast iron fry pan over medium heat on the stove or in an electric fry pan at 350 degrees Fahrenheit. Do not grease the surface. Bake the flat bread on a dry surface. Bake each piece for a minute or two on each side (until brown freckles appear).

When all of the flat bread has been baked, stack on an ungreased cookie sheet or a jelly roll pan and place in a 250-degree oven for an hour or until the flat bread is very crispy.

Remove from the oven. Allow to cool completely. Break into pieces. Store in a covered container. Serve spread with butter and sprinkled with sugar and cinnamon or just sugar.

****

Rommegrot (Sour Cream Pudding)
(Pronounced "rumma-grout")

The Norwegians ate quite a lot of dairy-based foods. Perhaps that's because most of them were dairy farmers. My mother did not especially care for Rommegrot, but when I came across a recipe in an old cookbook, she confirmed that's how it was made. You can mix raisins in with it, if you like.

> **1 cup sour cream**
> **1/4 cup flour**
> **2 cups whole milk (or cream)**
> **1/2 teaspoon salt**
> **1/2 to 3/4 cup sugar**
> **raisins (if desired)**
> **cinnamon**
> **butter**

Measure sour cream into a heavy saucepan, and over low heat, stir and heat until the sour cream starts to boil. Boil and continue stirring for a couple of minutes. Remove from the burner.

In a small mixing bowl or a cup, mix the 1/4 cup flour with a small amount of milk until it forms a smooth paste. Stir in the salt. Gradually stir in another half to 1 cup of milk, then stir the flour and milk mixture into the rest of the milk.

Gradually stir the milk and flour mixture into the sour cream. Return the saucepan to the burner and, over low-medium to medium heat, cook and stir until the pudding thickens. Just before removing the pudding from the burner, stir in the sugar. If you want a sweeter pudding, use 3/4 of a cup, otherwise use a 1/2 cup. If you want raisins, stir them in now. If you really like the taste of cinnamon, stir a 1/2 teaspoon of cinnamon into the pudding.

Serve warm sprinkled with sugar and cinnamon and a couple of dabs of butter.

Note: This reminds me of sour cream raisin pie or sour cream raisin bars—without the pie crust or without the crust part of the bars.

****

Norwegian Meatballs and Gravy

I am calling this recipe "Norwegian Meatballs and Gravy" because this is how my mother made meatballs and gravy. My mother generally used milk when she made any kind of gravy. Except for turkey gravy at Thanksgiving, but my sister usually made the gravy for Thanksgiving. Adding nutmeg to the meatballs is a "Norwegian" thing to do.

1/2 cup chopped onion
1 1/2 to 2 pounds ground beef
1/2 cup dry bread crumbs (or crushed saltine crackers)
1/4 cup milk
1 egg
1/2 to 1 teaspoon salt (if you use salted saltine crackers, use 1/2 teaspoon of salt, unless you like meatballs more on the salty side)
1/4 teaspoon pepper
1/2 teaspoon nutmeg

Measure the bread crumbs or cracker crumbs into a mixing bowl. Pour the milk over the crumbs and let sit for a few minutes. Beat in the egg. Add the ground beef, onion, salt, pepper and nutmeg. Mix until thoroughly combined. (I use my hands for this process.)

Melt a few tablespoons of shortening into a skillet. Make the meatballs about the size of a small egg. Fry in the shortening over medium heat until browned and the meatballs are cooked through (about 20 minutes or so, depending on how big you make your meatballs). Turn several times while cooking. Cover the pan in between turning the meatballs.

To make gravy:
Remove the meatballs and set aside. Melt a quarter cup of butter in the pan and stir into the meat drippings. Add a quarter cup of flour. Stir into the butter and meat drippings and cook over medium heat until bubbly. Slowly pour 2 cups of milk into the pan, stirring while you pour. Stir constantly and cook until the gravy thickens. If the gravy seems too thick, add milk by the tablespoon and cook until it reaches desired consistency. Add salt to taste.

Add the meatballs to the gravy and stir gently until the meatballs are coated. Heat through.

Serve with mashed potatoes. Or if you would rather—serve over cooked egg noodles or brown rice.

****

Sandbakelse
(The Easy Way)

Pronounced "sun-buckles"— traditionally, these Norwegian cookies are made in little fluted tins. My mother would never make sandbakelse because she said they were too much work. More recently, a friend of mine, who also is of Norwegian heritage, says she only makes a few in tins for Christmas "just because" and then rolls the rest of the dough into balls and bakes them that way. What a great idea! They are delicious!

3/4 cup butter
3/4 cup sugar
1 egg
2 cups flour
1/2 teaspoon salt
1/2 teaspoon almond extract
1/2 cup of slivered almonds chopped fine

Measure the butter and sugar into a mixing bowl and cream together. Beat in the egg. Add the flour, salt, almond extract and chopped almonds. Stir until thoroughly combined.

Roll dough into balls by small teaspoonfuls, press gently with a flat-bottomed water glass dipped in sugar and bake on an ungreased cookie sheet at 350 degrees Fahrenheit for 12 or 13 minutes or until cookies are fairly crisp.

To make traditional sandbakelse:
Pack dough into sandbakelse molds about 1/8 inch thick on the bottom and sides of mold. Place on a cookie sheet and bake at 350 degrees Fahrenheit for 12 or 15 minutes until the cookies are crispy. Allow to cool. Carefully tap the molds to loosen the cookies. Good luck!

****

Sweet Soup (Sot Suppe) Recipe

When my mother was a child, sweet soup was a traditional part of Christmas Eve, served cold with julekake, lefse, Christmas bread, or open-faced sandwiches. Sweet Soup is made with dried fruit and tapioca. Here is how my mother told me to make sot suppe.

6 cups water
1/3 cup sugar
1 tablespoon quick-cooking tapioca
1/4 to 1/2 teaspoon cinnamon (depending upon how well you like the taste of cinnamon; you can also use a cinnamon stick)
2 cups dried fruit (use any kind you like: apples, apricots, peaches or a mixture of dried fruit)
1 cup raisins (dark or golden)
1 cup dried prunes
1 tablespoon lemon juice (you can also use 1 teaspoon of dried lemon rind or several slices of fresh lemon)

In a medium saucepan, combine the sugar, tapioca, cinnamon and water. Bring to boiling, stirring constantly. Stir in fruit (including the lemon if you're using sliced lemon) and heat to boiling again. Cover. Simmer for 15 minutes, or until the fruit is tender.

After the fruit is tender, if you're using lemon juice, stir in the lemon juice (or teaspoon of dried lemon rind). Serve either cold or warm, depending upon your preference. If you use a sliced lemon, remove the lemon rind before serving.

For a light afternoon 'Norwegian' lunch (after hiking, sledding, snowshoeing or cross-country skiing), serve sweet soup with Julekake or Christmas bread, Christmas cookies, open-faced sandwiches, and a variety of sliced cheeses.

Sweet Soup is good in the summertime, too, when it's hot outside.

From the book written about Christmas on a "Norwegian" dairy farm:
Christmas In Dairyland (True Stories from a Wisconsin Farm)

****

Salads
&
Salad Dressings

Ambrosia

A neighbor of ours used to make this when I was a kid. I thought it was wonderful! Still do.

3 large oranges (peeled and cut into small pieces or sliced thin, whichever you like)
1 20-ounce can of chunk pineapple (drained)
1 cup shredded coconut

Arrange the orange pieces in the bottom of a serving bowl. Add the drained pineapple. Sprinkle 1 cup of coconut over the pineapple. Refrigerate until chilled. Stir before serving.

Serve in small sherbet dishes or six-ounce glasses.

****

Apple-Carrot Salad

If you like raisins, you can also add a cup of raisins to the salad. If the salad seems too dry, add a little more sour cream or mayonnaise. If you want a salad with more of a tart flavor, add a little more vinegar.

3 cups chopped apples
2 cups shredded carrots
1 1/2 cups chopped walnuts
2 tablespoons mayonnaise
1/2 cup sour cream
1/4 teaspoon salt
1/2 cup sugar
1 teaspoon cider vinegar (or a flavored vinegar if you wish; I like raspberry)
1 cup of raisins (if desired)

Measure the mayonnaise, sour cream, salt, sugar and vinegar into a small bowl. Mix thoroughly. Add more sour cream, mayonnaise, sugar or vinegar to taste. Chop the apples and shred the carrots. Put into a larger mixing bowl. Spoon the dressing over the salad and stir until thoroughly combined. Add 1 cup of raisins if desired.

****

Blue Cheese Dressing

Blue cheese salad dressing is my favorite. The nice thing about making your own blue cheese dressing is that you know just how much blue cheese is actually in the dressing. Sometimes I have gotten blue cheese dressing at restaurants and wondered what had happened to the blue cheese.

2 cups sour cream
2 teaspoons vinegar (any flavor you like)
1/2 teaspoon garlic salt
1 teaspoon sugar
1 teaspoon celery seed
1/4 teaspoon pepper
1 cup crumbled blue cheese

Measure the sour cream, vinegar, garlic salt, sugar, celery seed and pepper into a mixing bowl. Stir until thoroughly combined. Fold in the crumbled blue cheese.

****

Classic Coleslaw Dressing

When I was growing up, my dad loved coleslaw—and loved to make it. In the "good old days," Dad would grate the cabbage by hand that he had grown in our garden and would make his own dressing for the coleslaw. Nowadays, I use the preshredded coleslaw mix that has carrots and red cabbage in addition to the green cabbage. Dad never wrote down his coleslaw dressing recipe, but the one I developed myself is awfully close.

1 egg
1/2 teaspoon dry mustard
1/2 teaspoon sugar
1/2 teaspoon salt
2 tablespoons of vinegar
1 cup of salad oil (I like to use Canola oil; olive oil would work, too)
1/3 cup sugar
1 tablespoon vinegar

Put the egg, mustard, 1/2 teaspoon sugar, 1/2 teaspoon salt and 2 tablespoons of vinegar in a narrow, deep mixing bowl. Add 1/4 cup of the oil. Mix with an electric mixer on high for 30 seconds, then, while still beating with the mixer on high, pour in the remaining oil in a thin stream. Continue beating for several more minutes after all of the oil has been added. Total mixer time will be about 10 minutes.

Add 1/3 cup sugar and 1 tablespoon vinegar. Mix on high for another minute or so.

One recipe makes enough coleslaw dressing for 2 one-pound bags of coleslaw mix. If you don't use all of the dressing at one time, store the rest in the refrigerator in a covered container.

****

Cottage Cheese Fruit Salad

Cottage cheese salads and fruit salads were a staple food when I was a kid. This one is quick and easy.

1 eight-ounce container of cottage cheese
1 three-ounce package of flavored gelatin (any flavor you like, Jell-O or another brand)
1 regular can of crushed pineapple

Note: Instead of pineapple, fruit cocktail and/or mandarin oranges also can be used.

Dump the cottage cheese into a mixing bowl. Sprinkle the dry Jell-O over the cottage cheese and mix thoroughly. Stir in the can of crushed pineapple. Refrigerate for an hour or two before serving.

****

Cranberry-Orange Salad

This is another recipe that is very old and dates back to when I was growing up on the farm. It's good at any time of the year, but it makes an especially good salad at Thanksgiving.

2 three-ounce or 1 six-ounce package of raspberry flavored gelatin (Jell-O or another brand)
2 eleven-ounce cans of Mandarin oranges (drained)
1 20-ounch can of crushed pineapple
2 cups of cranberry sauce
1/4 to 1/2 cup of sugar (if you want a sweeter salad, use a 1/2 cup of sugar)

Dissolve the Jell-O in 1 cup of boiling water. Add 1/2 cup cold water. Drain the Mandarin oranges and cut into small pieces. If a "softer" salad is desired, stir in the Mandarin orange juice. Otherwise, just stir in the orange pieces and the crushed pineapple (and drink the Mandarin orange juice!). Measure the cranberry sauce into a small bowl and stir in the sugar. Mix the cranberries into the Jell-O mixture. Put into a serving bowl and refrigerate until set.

Serve with whipped cream, if desired.

****

Cucumber Salad (Norwegian Style)

In case you missed it in the "Norwegian" section, here is the recipe again for the type of cucumber salad we ate when I was a kid and we had plenty of cucumbers in the garden.

1/2 cup water
1/2 cup vinegar
1/2 cup white sugar
1/4 to 1/2 teaspoon salt
1/4 teaspoon ground black pepper
3 to 4 large cucumbers

Measure the water, vinegar, sugar, salt and pepper into a saucepan and bring to a boil.

Scrub the cucumbers. Cut off the bitter ends of the cucumbers. Do not peel the cucumbers. Cut into thin slices. Put the slices into a bowl and pour the hot liquid over the cucumbers. Let cool and then chill in the refrigerator. Serve when completely chilled.

****

5-Minute Fruit Salad

If you don't want to use grapes, the salad is good without them, too. (My husband really likes this salad with grapes.)

2 apples (cut into small pieces)
1 cup of grapes
3 tablespoons lemon juice
2-3 tablespoons orange marmalade
1/2 cup coconut

Cut 2 apples into small pieces (do not pare the apples; apple peelings are a good source of fiber and pectin; plus, the apple peel will give color to your salad). Put the apples into a medium mixing bowl. Wash the grapes and add to the apples.

Add 3 tablespoons lemon juice to the apples and grapes. Mix thoroughly. Add 2 to 3 tablespoons orange marmalade (or to taste) and 1/2 cup coconut. Mix thoroughly.

****

Freezer Coleslaw

You can serve this recipe without freezing the coleslaw or you can make it up ahead of time (such as before Thanksgiving or Christmas dinner) and store it in the refrigerator or the freezer until you're ready to use it. My dad grew cabbage in the garden, and my mother loved this recipe because it could be made ahead of time.

**1 medium head of cabbage OR 2 to 3 packages of shredded cabbage
(Ever since I scraped my knuckles raw grating cabbage for 150 people for a church dinner, I have preferred to use the shredded cabbage you can buy at the grocery store!)
3 sticks of celery chopped
1 teaspoon of celery seed
1/2 green pepper chopped (optional)**

Boil the following for 1 minute:
**1/2 cup white vinegar
1/2 cup water
2 cups sugar
1/4 teaspoon salt**

Put the cabbage, celery, celery seed and green pepper into a large mixing bowl. Pour the hot, boiled mixture over the cabbage, celery and green pepper.

If it seems like the coleslaw is much too soupy, which will depend much upon the moisture content of the cabbage you are using, add the third package of shredded cabbage. If you are going to freeze the coleslaw, however, you want the coleslaw to be covered with liquid.

At this point, you can let the coleslaw sit in the refrigerator for 1 to 2 hours or overnight and serve, or you can put it into containers and freeze. The coleslaw will keep in the refrigerator for 1 to 2 weeks.

Note: this recipe works very well for red cabbage, too, and makes a pretty side dish.

****

Heavenly Apple Salad

This recipe makes a large bowl of apple salad, perfect for family gatherings or other events. If you make this salad to take to a family gathering or church event, don't be surprised if there's none left by the end of the afternoon. This salad is deeeee-licious!

1 20 ounce can of crushed pineapple
1 cup sugar
1/4 cup flour
2 tablespoons vinegar
1 large container of Cool Whip (or a similar topping)
1 24-ounce jar of dry roasted peanuts
6 to 8 apples (depending upon the size of the apples)

Measure the crushed pineapple, sugar, flour and vinegar into a medium saucepan and cook over medium heat until thick. When cooled to room temperature, place in the refrigerator for several hours or overnight.

Cut the apples into small pieces. Add the pineapple mixture. Stir in Cool Whip (or other topping) and all but 1 cup of the peanuts. Mix thoroughly. Sprinkle the remaining peanuts on top.

****

Italian Pasta Salad

Use whatever vegetables you like in this salad. If you've got fresh onions from your garden, or tomatoes, or snow peas — add some of those, too. This makes a large salad of 8 to 10 servings. Make a half a recipe for a smaller salad. Pasta salads were another staple when I was a kid growing up on our farm.

1 12-ounce package of rotini pasta (I like to use the Wacky Mac colored pasta because it makes a pretty salad)
1 six-ounce can of black olives sliced into small pieces
4 cups of raw broccoli
2 to 3 carrots cut into small pieces
1 bottle of Italian salad dressing

Cook the pasta, drain and rinse with cold water. Dump into a large mixing bowl. Add the chopped broccoli, sliced carrots and the black olives. Add other vegetables, too, if you like (sweet bell peppers, onions and Roma tomatoes work well). Season with Italian bottled dressing to suit your taste. Mix thoroughly.

Note: you can also add 1 to 2 cups of cottage cheese to the salad or 1 to 2 cups of cheddar cheese cut into cubes.

****

Macaroni Salad
(Tuna Noodle Pea Salad)

This salad was a regular in the summer when I was growing up on our farm when it was too hot to cook and too hot to eat hot food. Nowadays, I don't use tuna in it. My husband doesn't really care for tuna fish, so I add more cheese. You can also use chicken or turkey cut into small pieces.

4 cups to 6 cups cooked macaroni (or spiral macaroni or egg noodles or Wacky Mac)
1 medium onion, chopped
1 to 2 cups cubed cheddar cheese
1 can tuna
1 can of peas, drained (or 1 to 2 cups of fresh peas cooked)
1 can of black olives (sliced)
Ranch or Blue Cheese salad dressing
Mayonnaise

Cook the macaroni, drain, rinse until cool. Dump into a large mixing bowl.

Add the chopped onion, cheddar cheese, tuna (if desired) (or chicken or turkey) and black olives (if desired) and the peas.

Stir in Ranch or Blue Cheese dressing and mayonnaise to taste.

****

Overnight Lemon Pineapple Salad

This is a very old recipe we used when I was a kid, and it is delicious. The nice thing about it is that you put it together the night before. If you are making it for a family gathering or another event, it's "one less thing" you will have to do the next day!

2 egg yolks
1 cup pineapple juice (use the juice from the can of crushed pineapple)
pinch of salt
1/2 cup sugar
1 tablespoon corn starch

1 20-ounce can of crushed pineapple (drained)
2 tablespoons lemon juice
1 cup cream (whipped)
1/3 cup sugar
1 1/2 cups of miniature marshmallows
Maraschino cherries (optional)

Put the egg yolks into a saucepan. Stir in the pineapple juice and beat with a fork until mixed. Measure the sugar, cornstarch and salt into a cup or a small dish. Mix until thoroughly combined. Stir into the egg yolk. Cook over medium heat until thick, stirring constantly (a couple of minutes). Let the mixture cool for 20 to 30 minutes.

Put the crushed pineapple and lemon juice into a mixing bowl. Stir until thoroughly combined. Spoon the egg yolk and pineapple juice mixture over the pineapple and lemon juice and stir.

Whip the cream with an electric mixer until it begins to thicken. Gradually add the sugar while whipping, 1 tablespoon at a time. Continue to whip until it reaches the right consistency (a couple of minutes). Stir in the marshmallows.

Fold the whipped cream and marshmallow mixture into the pineapple mixture. Spoon into a serving bowl. Place in the refrigerator overnight. Garnish with Maraschino cherries if desired before serving.

* * * * * * * * * * * * * * * * * * * *

Parfait Fruit Salad

This fruit salad also was a standby when I was a kid. My mother always added bananas to the fruit salad, too. I like bananas, but my husband does not. He had an unfortunate experience with bananas when he was a small child.

2 11-ounce cans of mandarin oranges
1 20-ounce can of chunk pineapple
1 20-ounce can of fruit cocktail
1 20 ounce can of sliced peaches
1 three-ounce package of instant vanilla pudding
1 to 2 cups walnuts (chopped walnuts or walnuts broken into pieces)
1 medium or 2 small apples cut into small pieces
1 cup of grapes (optional)
1 jar maraschino cherries (optional)
1 to 2 bananas cut into pieces (optional)
Cool Whip (or a similar topping) (if needed)

Drain the fruit and dump the fruit into a mixing bowl. Add the apple and banana pieces (if desired). Sprinkle the dry pudding mix over the fruit and fold in until thoroughly combined. Refrigerate for several hours until chilled or refrigerate overnight.

Before serving, stir in the walnuts and maraschino cherries (if desired). If the salad seems too dry, stir in Cool Whip to taste.

For a lighter version, use sugar-free pudding mix and fruit canned in light syrup.

****

Western Ranch Dressing

When I was a kid, we raised lettuce, onions, radishes, carrots, tomatoes and cucumbers in our garden. We often ate salad with dinner and with supper. My sister sometimes made the dressing. Mom preferred homemade salad dressing over buying it in the store, because with five hungry people eating salads, she would have had to buy it by the gallon! She always had these ingredients on hand.

1/3 cup sugar
1 cup salad oil (Canola, olive, corn, grapeseed — whatever you prefer)
1/2 cup catsup
1/2 cup vinegar (Cider vinegar or clear) (experiment with other flavored vinegars, too)
1/2 to 1 teaspoon garlic salt (depending on how salty you want your salad dressing)
1 small or medium onion chopped fine

Measure all ingredients into a quart jar. Cover. Shake well until the sugar is dissolved. If you want a sweeter salad dressing, add more sugar by the tablespoon. Shake again until the sugar is dissolved. Chill. Store in the refrigerator.

If this salad dressing is made up ahead of time and is refrigerated overnight, it has a better flavor. Keeps in the refrigerator quite well. Shake the jar again before pouring the dressing over your salad.

****

Raspberries and Cream Salad

This recipe is so good that if you make it for a special occasion (birthday, graduation, anniversary, holiday or family dinner) don't expect any leftovers! My husband loves raspberries, so of course, this is one of his favorite salads. I have made this salad for church dinners and funerals, too.

2 6-ounce packages of raspberry flavored gelatin (Jell-O or another brand)
2 cans raspberry pie filling
1 cup sugar
1 12-ounce container of Cool Whip (or another similar topping)
1 8-ounce package of cream cheese
2 cups crushed pretzels
1 cup crushed walnuts
2 tablespoons sugar
1/4 cup melted butter

Prepare the raspberry Jell-O with boiling water according to package directions. Mix in the raspberry pie filling. Pour into a serving bowl and place in the refrigerator until set. (Instead of a serving bowl, you can make the salad in a 9x13 cake pan if you wish.)

Allow the Cool Whip (or other topping) and the cream cheese to warm to room temperature (or warm for a few seconds in the microwave). Whip the topping, cream cheese and 1 cup of sugar until smooth and thoroughly mixed. Spread over the Jell-O mixture.

Melt the butter in a saucepan. Add 2 tablespoons sugar, the crushed pretzels and crushed walnuts. Stir thoroughly. Sprinkle over the topping/raspberry Jell-O.

Keep refrigerated until you are ready to serve.

Note: I have also made a light version of the recipe and used sugar-free gelatin, fat-free topping and fat-free cream cheese.

****

Strawberry Parfait Jell-O Salad

For an added touch, serve on a bed of leaf lettuce. Or line the bottom and sides of a serving bowl with leaf lettuce and put the salad on top of the lettuce. I grow Red Sails lettuce in my garden, and the salad is especially pretty with Red Sails.

2 3-ounce packages (or 1 6-ounce package) of strawberry flavored gelatin (Jell-O or another brand)
4 ounces of Strawberry Cool Whip (you can also use just plain Cool Whip or a similar topping)
4 ounces of soft cream cheese
1/2 cup of powdered sugar
fresh strawberries (optional)

Put the dry Jell-O in a mixing bowl and add 2 cups of boiling water. Stir until gelatin is dissolved. Add 1 cup of cold water.

Pour into an ungreased 9x13 pan and put in the refrigerator until set.

When the gelatin is set, use a knife to cut across the pan at 1/2-inch intervals. Also cut at 1/2-inch intervals the length of the pan. Use a spoon to scoop out the cubes of gelatin into a mixing bowl.

In a separate mixing bowl, measure out the Cool Whip, cream cheese and powdered sugar. Use an electric mixer to whip until smooth.

Stir the Cool Whip/cream cheese mixture into the gelatin cubes. Serve on a bed of leaf lettuce or in a bowl lined with leaf lettuce. Decorate with sliced strawberries, if desired. You can also decorate with sliced kiwi fruit.

****

Sweet and Sour Salad Dressing

This dressing works very well either on cabbage or on lettuce. Keeps well in the refrigerator for about a month. You can also use it to marinate sliced cucumbers or tomatoes.

1/2 cup water
1 cup sugar
1 cup of vinegar (either white or cider or experiment with other flavors. I like raspberry vinegar)
1 teaspoon celery seed
1/2 teaspoon ground mustard
1/4 to 1/2 teaspoon salt (depending on how salty you want it)

Measure all ingredients into a quart jar or another container that seals very tightly. Shake until the sugar is dissolved. Chill. Store in the refrigerator.

****

Thousand Island Dressing

If you use celery seed and onion flakes, this is an easy, quick recipe.

1 cup mayonnaise
1/4 teaspoon salt
1/4 teaspoon pepper
1 teaspoon Worcestershire sauce
1/4 to 1/2 cup catsup (depending on how much tomato flavor you want in your dressing)
2 tablespoons of sweet pickle relish
1/3 cup of finely chopped celery (or 1 teaspoon celery seed)
1 tablespoon to 1/4 cup chopped onion, depending on how well you like onion (you can also use dried onion flakes, if you want; if you use onion flakes, use 1 tablespoon)

Measure all ingredients into a mixing bowl and stir until thoroughly combined. Store in the refrigerator in an air-tight container and chill. Keeps in the refrigerator for a couple of weeks.

****

Three-Bean Salad

This is another of my favorites. Nowadays I don't get to eat it very often, though, because my husband does not like kidney beans in any way, shape or form.

1 can of green beans (either regular or French style)
1 can of wax beans
1 can of red kidney beans
1 medium onion
1/2 cup green pepper or sweet red bell pepper (optional)
1/2 cup sugar
1/3 cup salad oil
1/2 cup vinegar
1 teaspoon salt
1/2 teaspoon celery seed (optional)

Peel the onion, cut into slices and separate the slices into rings. Place the rings in a mixing bowl.

Drain the green beans, wax beans and kidney beans and add to the mixing bowl. Add green pepper or sweet red bell pepper if desired.

Measure the sugar, salad oil, vinegar, salt and celery seed (if desired) into a small mixing bowl and stir until the sugar is dissolved. Pour over the beans and onions and stir gently until thoroughly mixed. Taste. If salad is too tart, add more sugar by tablespoons. If salad is too sweet, add more vinegar a few drops at a time until it suits your taste.

Refrigerate for several hours or overnight. Stir again before serving.

****

A Tip for Making Fresh Tossed Salad During the Winter

I would hate to think about how many bags of salad lettuce I have thrown out only partially used because the lettuce has started to turn slimy and brown. If I buy a bag of salad lettuce, and we don't eat it all in the first day or two, it starts to go bad.

I don't have the time or the inclination to run to the grocery store every day for fresh lettuce, so this is a problem for me. The closest grocery store is seven mile away. During the summer when lettuce is growing in my garden, it's not a problem, of course. But it's definitely a problem the rest of the year.

I solved that problem by using shredded cabbage for tossed salads instead. I discovered that bags of shredded cabbage keep in the refrigerator for up to two weeks (or sometimes more if the cabbage was really fresh when it was shredded), even if the bag has been opened. I use the cabbage the same way I would use bagged lettuce.

Try it and see what you think. Add fresh carrots, bell peppers, olives, fresh onion, sunflower seeds, tomatoes—whatever you like to eat in a fresh salad. Top with your favorite salad dressing.

Another benefit is that I heard a physician on public radio a few years ago talking about the fact that cabbage contains a natural ingredient which keeps breast cancer cells from dividing.

If you can't stand cabbage in any way, shape or form, I would not recommend using it in a salad. But if you like cabbage, give it a try for your tossed salads.

****

Vegetables

Beets in Orange Sauce

Dad grew lots of beets in our garden on the farm. Beets in Orange Sauce (and Harvard Beets) were summertime vegetables served at dinner or supper when fresh beets were available from the garden. Later on in the summer, my mother would make pickled beets, also one of Dad's favorites, and we would then have pickled beets for the rest of the year.

5 medium fresh beets (or 1 quart/pound of canned beets drained)
2 tablespoons cornstarch
2 tablespoons brown sugar
1/2 teaspoon salt
2 teaspoons of dried ground orange peel (or finely shredded orange peel from a fresh orange)
3/4 cup orange juice
1 tablespoon vinegar

Cook the beets and peel and cut into slices. Set aside. (Do not peel fresh beets before you cook them. Do not cut off the stem or the root, either.)

Measure the brown sugar, cornstarch, orange peel and salt into a fry pan (large enough to hold the sliced beets) and stir until thoroughly combined. Stir in the orange juice and vinegar. Stirring constantly, cook over medium heat until the mixture boils. Cook until thick (a minute or so). Add beet slices. Stir and heat through.

****

Creamed Vegetables

This recipe was a regular during the summer when I was a kid when carrots, green beans, peas and new potatoes were fresh from the garden. We often ate sliced tomatoes, sliced cucumbers and creamed vegetables served over new potatoes for our summertime dinners along with slices of homemade bread spread with butter. Fresh whole milk from our cows and butter from the creamery made it especially tasty!

My favorite was carrots, beans and peas mixed together. We didn't always have peas, though, because Dad only raised "a few." One year my mother spent a tremendous amount of time shelling peas and then canning them. Every jar of peas turned sour, and she refused to can peas after that. In the spring, Mom would say, "Roy, you're not planting peas in the garden, are you?" And Dad would say, "Nope. Just a few. Enough so we can pick some in the evening when we visit the garden." And then he would wink at me. Visiting the garden to see what had grown and what was a ripe was a ritual I shared with my dad in the evening when the milking was finished.

1/4 cup butter (or instead of butter and shortening, use 1/2 stick of butter)
1/4 shortening (lard or bacon fat works, too)
1/4 cup flour
1/2 teaspoon salt
2 cups milk
3 cups cooked vegetables

Melt the butter and shortening in a large skillet. Stir in the flour with a fork and cook for a few seconds until bubbly. Gradually stir in the milk. Continue cooking over medium heat, stirring constantly, until the mixture thickens. Stir in the vegetables and heat through.

Cheesy Creamed Vegetables: stir in 1 cup of shredded aged cheddar cheese and stir until the cheese melts before adding the vegetables.

****

Different Glazed Carrots

My husband loves this recipe for glazed carrots. Instead of brown sugar and butter, it uses fruit juice. It is a quick and easy recipe, too.

4 cups of cooked carrots (either fresh or frozen carrots; 4 cups of fresh carrots equals 4 to 6 medium to large carrots)
1 cup fruit juice (any kind of juice—pineapple, orange, cherry, apple, grape, cranberry, apricot; I have used V-8 Splash fruit juice, too.)
1 tablespoon cornstarch
1 tablespoon sugar (if you use cranberry juice, you might want to add 2 tablespoons of sugar)
1/4 teaspoon salt

Cook the carrots. Drain. Mix the cornstarch with a quarter cup of fruit juice and stir until smooth. Stir into the remaining juice. Stir in the sugar and salt until dissolved. Pour over the carrots and cook over medium heat, stirring constantly (a couple of minutes), until the sauce thickens.

****

Glazed Carrots

Glazed carrots were my favorite when I was growing up on our farm. My sister used to make them quite often for supper. And I still love them today!

4 cups of cooked carrots
1/2 cup brown sugar
1/4 cup butter
1/2 to 1 teaspoon grated orange peel (optional)
1/4 teaspoon salt

Melt the butter in a large skillet. Stir in the brown sugar and the orange peel (if desired). Cook over low to medium heat, stirring constantly, for about five minutes or until the mixture is thick and bubbly. If the mixture becomes too thick, stir in a tablespoon of warm water. Stir in the carrots and heat through.

****

Harvard Beets

I have to confess it was not until I was an adult that I found out these kinds of beets were called "Harvard Beets." Dad, whose mother was German, just called them "sweet and sour beets."

5 medium fresh beets (or 1 quart/pound of canned beets drained; save liquid)
1 tablespoon cornstarch
2 tablespoons sugar
1/2 teaspoon salt
2/3 cup water (or beet liquid from canned beets; add water if necessary to make 2/3 cup)
1/4 cup vinegar

Cook beets, peel and cut into slices. Set aside. (If you are cooking fresh beets, do not cut off the stem ends or the root ends before cooking.)

Measure sugar, cornstarch and salt into a frying pan (large enough to hold the sliced beets) and stir until thoroughly combined. Stir in the water (or beet juice) and vinegar. Stirring constantly, cook over medium heat until mixture boils. Cook until thick (a minute or so). Add beet slices.

****

Onion Vegetable Dip

My husband, like many men, thinks raw vegetables are bland and are not really food at all. This vegetable dip makes raw carrots, celery, broccoli, cauliflower and other vegetables just a bit more interesting. And the recipe is easy, too!

1 cup sour cream (or light sour cream)
3 teaspoons onion soup mix (or to taste)
2 tablespoons dried onion

Mix all ingredients thoroughly. Refrigerate for one hour before serving.

****

Sauerkraut in Jars

Making sauerkraut in jars can get kind of messy, but if you like sauerkraut, it's a fun and interesting project to make your own. It's fairly easy, too, especially if you use packages of shredded cabbage that you bought at the store. My dad's German grandmother made sauerkraut in crocks, but you probably don't need or want that much sauerkraut—and good luck finding the crocks, anyway. If you find "real" crocks at an auction, be prepared to get into a bidding war with the antique dealers or someone else who really wants those crocks.

5 pounds shredded cabbage
3 1/2 tablespoons pickling salt
4 or 5 canning jars with lids and rings (more or less, depends on how tightly you pack the jars)

Measure the cabbage and salt into a large mixing bowl and stir thoroughly.

Pack the cabbage into quart jars. Add cold water if necessary to cover the cabbage. Screw the lids down but not tight.

Put the jars on several layers of newspaper in a warm, dark place. (If you've got space next to your refrigerator or freezer, these two appliances generate plenty of heat.)

Cover the jars with several layers of newspaper. The jars will ferment for 3 or 4 days. When fermentation is finished (jars are no longer bubbling over), wipe off jars, tighten the covers.

Store in a cool place (either in your basement or in your refrigerator). The sauerkraut will be ready in 4 to 6 weeks.

****

Sweet Corn for the Freezer

Dad always raised at least a couple of rows of sweet corn at the edge of the field corn on our farm. Our family liked sweet corn, and this is how my mother would freeze it. This recipe is delicious!

Husk the sweet corn, pick off the silk and rinse the cobs.

Cut the raw corn off the cobs. (I use a jelly roll pan for cutting off the corn. I hold the cobs upright in the pan and let the corn fall into the jelly roll pan. I can cut off quite a few cobs before I have to dump the pan.)

Depending upon the size of the cobs, about 30 cobs will yield 4 quarts of corn.

Measure into a large kettle:
  4 quarts of corn
  3 cups water
  2 to 3 teaspoons of salt (if you like your corn salty, use 3 teaspoons, if you don't want as much salt, use 2 teaspoons)
  1 tablespoon sugar
  1 stick of butter (1/2 cup)

Stir all ingredients together, bring to a boil over medium-high heat and cook for 5 minutes, stirring occasionally. Let cool and put into freezer containers or freezer bags.

The important thing about sweet corn is to make sure it cools off relatively quickly. If the corn stays warm for too long, it can end up sour. I also use the jelly roll pan to cool off the corn before I put it in containers. I spoon the hot corn into the jelly roll pan and keep stirring it until it is cool enough to go into freezer containers or freezer bags. Then I put the corn into the freezer right away.

****

Taco Dip

I make this at Christmas, and it's always a big hit with the nieces and nephews (all grown up and married now), and my husband, too, of course. Serve with taco chips and/or with fresh vegetables.

2 8-ounce containers of sour cream
2 8-ounce containers of cream cheese
1 can of black olives
1 to 2 cups shredded cheddar cheese
1 jar of salsa (mild or hot, depending on your preference)

Let cream cheese warm to room temperature. Place the sour cream and cream cheese into a mixing bowl. Using an electric mixer, start out on low until the cream cheese and sour cream are combined, then whip on high for a minute or two. Add the salsa (to taste; use only a little or pour in the whole jar; it's up to you). Whip on high for a minute or two.

Stir in black olives and the cheddar cheese. Refrigerate. Serve chilled with any kind of taco chips and/or with fresh vegetables: carrot sticks, celery sticks, broccoli, cauliflower, green pepper, sweet red bell pepper—whatever you like.

If you want to get "really fancy" for a special get-together—spread the taco dip onto a large platter. Sprinkle shredded lettuce over the taco dip. Sprinkle more shredded cheddar cheese over the lettuce. Cut a can of olives into slices. Chop some tomatoes. Sprinkle the olives and tomatoes over the cheese.

****

Vinaigrette Tomatoes

If you like fresh tomatoes and you've got lots of them in your garden—or if you have a Farmers' Market close by—this is an easy (and delicious!) way to serve tomatoes. In fact, it was my mother's favorite way to eat fresh tomatoes.

12 thick tomato slices
1 cup olive oil or canola oil
1/3 cup vinegar (white, cider, raspberry, or any flavor you like)
1 teaspoon crushed or dried oregano leaves
1/2 teaspoon salt
1/4 teaspoon pepper
1/2 teaspoon dry mustard
2 cloves of crushed garlic or a 1/2 teaspoon garlic powder (or garlic powder to taste)

Arrange tomato slices in a shallow baking dish that has a cover. Pour the oil into a jar. Add the vinegar, oregano, salt, pepper, mustard and garlic. Cover the jar with a lid. Shake until all ingredients are blended.

Pour the oil and vinegar mixture over the tomatoes. Cover the dish. Chill the tomatoes for 2 or 3 hours. While the tomatoes are chilling, spoon some of the dressing over the tomatoes a couple of times.

When you've eaten all of the tomato slices, you can save the dressing for the next batch of tomato slices.

****

Zesty Green Beans

When I was growing up, we often ate green beans for supper with just a tablespoon of butter on each serving. My husband thinks that's a "bland" way to eat green beans. This recipe for green beans is my husband's favorite.

1 can of green beans (or an equivalent package of frozen green beans)
2 tablespoons canola oil (or olive oil)
1 tablespoon vinegar
2 tablespoons chopped onion (I have also used shallots, which gives the recipe a stronger flavor)
garlic powder to taste or 1 clove of fresh garlic chopped
1/2 cup crushed saltine crackers (my husband really likes the crackers in the green beans, so I use 1 cup of crushed crackers)
1/4 cup Parmesan cheese

In an ungreased casserole dish, mix the beans, Canola or olive oil, vinegar, chopped onion and garlic. Add the crackers and Parmesan cheese and stir until the crackers and cheese are mixed in well.

Bake at 350 degrees Fahrenheit for 30 minutes or until heated through. Sprinkle more Parmesan cheese over each serving, if desired.

****

Measurements
&
Substitutions

Measurements

3 teaspoons = 1 tablespoon

2 tablespoons = 1/8 cup

4 tablespoons = 1/4 cup

8 tablespoons = 1/2 cup

16 tablespoons = 1 cup

5 tablespoons + 1 teaspoon = 1/3 cup

1/2 cup + 2 tablespoons = 5/8 cup

3/4 cup + 2 tablespoons = 7/8 cup

2 tablespoons of liquid = 1 ounce

1/2 cup liquid = 4 ounces

1 cup liquid = 8 ounces

1 pound = 16 ounces

2 cups = 1 pint

4 cups = 1 quart

2 pints = 1 quart

4 quarts = 1 gallon

1 pint = 1 pound

8 quarts = 1 peck

4 pecks = 1 bushel

32 quarts = 1 bushel

Pinch = as much as can be taken between the tips of the fingers and your thumb

****

Equivalents

Apples: 4 cups of sliced or chopped = 4 medium apples

Banana: A cup of mashed = 3 medium

Brown sugar: 2 1/4 cups = 1 pound

Butter: 1 pound = 2 cups or 4 sticks

Cabbage: 4 cups shredded = 1 pound

Cracker crumbs: 1 cup = 24 saltine crackers

Coconut: 3 cups = 1/2 pound

Cranberries: 4 cups = 1 pound

Crushed cornflakes or other flake-type cereal: 1 cup = 3 cups uncrushed

Egg whites: 1 cup = 8 to 10 egg whites

Egg yolks: 1 cup = 12 to 14 egg yolks

Flour: 4 cups = 1 pound

Lemon: 1 whole = 3 to 4 tablespoons of lemon juice

Macaroni: 4 cups cooked = 1 eight-ounce package

Orange: 1 whole = 6 to 8 tablespoons juice

Potatoes: 4 cups sliced or diced = 4 medium potatoes

Powdered Sugar: 3 1/2 to 4 cups = 1 pound

Rice: 3 1/3 cups cooked = 1 cup uncooked rice

****

~ Acknowledgements ~

Thank you to my husband, Randy Simpson, for designing the book cover and the website (www.ruralroute2cookbook.com).

Thank you, too, to my mother (may she rest in peace), my sister, Loretta—and even Dad (may he also rest in peace)—for teaching me how to cook. Dad taught, too, me how much fun it is growing food in my own garden. We always had a garden when I was growing up on our small family dairy farm in west central Wisconsin. As far as he was concerned, it was truly a miracle that a tiny seed put into the soil would grow up to be a specific type of plant that could be used as food and that could make its own seeds. He was right, of course.

****

~ About the Author ~

LeAnn R. Ralph is a newspaper reporter who lives in west central Wisconsin. She earned an undergraduate degree in English with a Writing Emphasis and a Master of Arts in Teaching English from the University of Wisconsin—Whitewater. She lives in the house her folks built when they retired from farming and shares her home with her husband, Randy, assorted cats, a Shetland Sheepdog named Pixie and her two horses, Isabelle and Kajun.

Besides *The Rural Route 2 Cookbook*, LeAnn also is the author of the books *Where the Green Grass Grows* (trade paperback; October 2006; $13.95*)*, *Cream of the Crop* (trade paperback; September 2005; $13.95) *Give Me a Home Where the Dairy Cows Roam* (trade paperback; September 2004; $13.95); *Christmas in Dairyland (True Stories from a Wisconsin Farm)* (trade paperback; August 2003; $13.95) and *Preserve Your Family History (A Step-by-Step Guide for Writing Oral Histories* (Trade paperback; August 2007; $12.95).

For more information about LeAnn, to read sample chapters from her books or to order books (FREE shipping!) visit her website—www.ruralroute2.com

****

~ How to Order More Books ~

Here's how to order more copies of *The Rural Route 2 Cookbook, Where the Green Grass Grows, Cream of the Crop, Give Me a Home Where the Dairy Cows Roam, Christmas in Dairyland* and *Preserve Your Family History (A Step-by-Step Guide for Interviewing Family Members and Writing Oral Histories)*:

• Order on the Internet through Booklocker.com
• Order on the Internet through Amazon.com or Barnes & Noble.
• Order through your local bookstore.
• Call LeAnn at (715) 308-6336.
• Write to LeAnn at E6689 970th Ave.; Colfax, WI 54730
• Order from LeAnn's website—www.ruralroute2.com

When you order books directly from the author (either by calling, writing or ordering through www.ruralroute2.com), you can request autographed copies with personalized inscriptions. Free shipping, too!

****

Book Reviews

Christmas in Dairyland (True Stories from a Wisconsin Farm)
(August 2003; ISBN 1-59113-366-1; $13.95; www.ruralroute2.com)

Christmas In Dairyland: True Stories From A Wisconsin Farm by LeAnn R. Ralph is a heartwarming anthology of true anecdotes of rural life on a Wisconsin dairy farm. Even though Wisconsin is still known as America's Dairyland, life on a family homestead is fast being replaced by corporate agribusiness, and the memories treasured in *Christmas In Dairyland* are quickly becoming unique milestones of an era needing to be preserved in thought and print for the sake of future generations. *Christmas In Dairyland* is simply wonderful reading and is a "must" for all Wisconsin public library collections.

James A. Cox, Editor-in-Chief
Midwest Book Review

****

~ Book Review ~

Give Me a Home Where the Dairy Cows Roam
(Oct. 2004; ISBN-1-59113-592-3; $13.95; www.ruralroute2.com)

Give Me A Home Where The Dairy Cows Roam is a collection of autobiographical stories drawn from author LeAnn Ralph's family dairy farm in Wisconsin in a time when small family farms were commonplace in the Badger State's rural countryside.

Now that we live in a time when approximately 85% of American family dairy farms have disappeared into suburban township developments or absorbed into agribusiness scale corporate farming enclaves, LeAnn takes us back some forty years ago into an era when dairy farming was a dawn-to-dusk life, seven days a week lifestyle that bonded parents and children with hard work and a sense of the land, animals, and homestead that is rapidly passing from today's expanding urban society.

More than just an autobiographical collection of anecdotal stories, *Give Me A Home Where The Dairy Cows Roam* is also enhanced with a recipe for making homemade ice cream without an ice cream maker and a recipe for "Norma's Homemade Bread". Highly recommended reading, *Give Me A Home Where The Dairy Cows Roam* should be on the shelves of every community library in Wisconsin.

James A. Cox, Editor-in-Chief
Midwest Book Review

****

~ Book Review ~

Cream Of The Crop: More True Stories Form A Wisconsin Farm
(October 2005; ISBN 1591138205; $13.95; www.ruralroute2.com)

Cream of the Crop is the third anthology of biographical and anecdotal stories by LeAnn Ralph about growing up on a Wisconsin dairy farm. In the 1960s there were more than 60,000 dairy farms in Wisconsin, in May of 2004 the Wisconsin Agricultural Statistics Service recorded the number of surviving dairy farms in the state at 15,591. The number has dropped even lower since then. That dairy farming reality is what helps to give LeAnn's deftly told stories their nostalgia for a rural lifestyle that is not-so-slowly disappearing in the Badger state. There are twenty short but immensely entertaining stories in this simply superb anthology. They range from "What's in a Name", to "She'll Be Comin' Round the Cornfield", to "Gertrude and Heathcliff", to the title story "Cream Of The Crop". LeAnn continues to write with a remarkable knack for making people and events come alive in the reader's imagination. Also very highly recommended are LeAnn's two earlier anthologies about life on the family farm in Wisconsin: *Give Me A Home Where The Dairy Cows Roam* (1591135923, $13.95) and *Christmas In Dairyland: True Stories From A Wisconsin Farm* (1591133661, $13.95).

James A. Cox, Editor-in-Chief
Midwest Book Review

****

Preserve Your Family History (A Step-by-Step Guide for Interviewing Family Members and Writing Oral Histories)
(July 2007; ISBN ISBN-13 978-1-60145-239-9; ISBN-10 1-60145-239-X $11.95;
www.ruralroute2.com)

"Preserve Your Family History: A Step-by-Step Guide For Interviewing Family Members And Writing Oral Histories" by LeAnn R. Ralph is a thoroughly 'user friendly' instruction manual specifically designed and written for non-specialist general readers who would like to capture the anecdotal histories of aging family members whether it would be for supplementing genealogical research, preserving stories and biographies for the benefit of future generations, or to simply learn about the life stories of family members while they are still able to relate them. "Preserve Your Family History" demonstrates that all that is needed is compiling a list of people to be interviewed, a set of questions to ask them, a tape recorder to preserve what is said, a pen and notepad to write on, a typewriter or computer to put it all down in writing, and above all else, a willingness to listen. The benefits of recording family members' oral histories and anecdotal recollections is that their experiences are the backdrop for your own history, the foundations for your own value system, opinions, and attitudes, a framework to explain how you fit into your own family structure. "Preserve Your Family History" is meant to be a 'consumable', that is, to be written in, selected pages photocopied, given to others to utilize in preparing for interviews, and shared with others in cooperative efforts to preserve family histories while those who lived and created that history are still with us. Also very highly recommended for personal reading, as well as Wisconsin community library collections, are LeAnn *Ralph's Christmas in Dairyland: True Stories from a Wisconsin Farm* (2003); *Give Me a Home Where the Diary Cows Roam* (2004); *Cream of the Crop: More True Stories from a Wisconsin Farm* (2005); and *Where The Green Grass Grows: True (Spring and Summer) Stories from a Wisconsin Farm* (2006).

James A. Cox, Editor-in-Chief
Midwest Book Review

LaVergne, TN USA
26 April 2010
180529LV00001B/1/P

9 781601 455925